MARK
Ralph P. Martin

KNOX PREACHING GUIDES
John H. Hayes, Editor

John Knox Press
ATLANTA

Library of Congress Cataloging in Publication Data

Martin, Ralph P.
  Mark.

  (Knox preaching guides)
  Bibliography: p.
  1. Bible. N.T. Mark—Commentaries. 2. Bible.
N.T. Mark—Homiletical use. I. Title. II. Series.
BS2585.3.M37   226'.307   81-82351
ISBN 0-8042-3234-2   AACR2

© copyright John Knox Press 1981
10 9 8 7 6 5 4 3 2 1
Printed in the United States of America
John Knox Press
Atlanta, Georgia 30365

Contents

MARK

Introduction

Mark the Storyteller

Mark's gospel has the reputation, in popular imagination and much pastoral use, of being the most straightforward of all the accounts of Jesus' earthly ministry. This estimate is understandable.

The readers are not faced with marvelous stories of angelic appearances at Jesus' nativity, and there is no hint of a virgin birth. Instead, Jesus bursts on the scene as a fully grown man (1:9), ready to commence his active work (1:14, 15). He was formerly the carpenter of Nazareth (6:3). Now he is a powerful wonderworker, exorcist and teacher who moves inexorably to his destiny in Jerusalem where, after the confession of Peter, "You are the Messiah" (8:29), he anticipates his rejection, suffering and death to be followed by a triumphant vindication (14:28, 16:7). But the resurrection is only partly described, and again angelic visitants are absent.

All this dramatic, high-tension narrative carries the reader with it and leaves us often breathless with Jesus' forceful decisions, quick actions, realistic responses to threatening situations, and the eventual climax in Jerusalem where the highpoint of the drama is reached. "Come away by yourselves to a lonely place, and rest a while" (6:31) is Jesus' invitation to the Twelve. Mark explains what is obvious to his audience: "Many were coming and going, and they had no leisure . . ."

(6:31, a verse only Mark records). The present-day reader may well feel caught up with the rapid pace of Jesus' activity and experience the disciples' exhaustion.

Whatever else this gospel is, it is a good story, told by a master raconteur who holds the readers' attention from start to finish. Dramatic recitations of Mark's gospel on the theater stage in our day (notably by Alec McCowen) have shown that this writing has lost none of its dramatic, gripping appeal.

Mark the Evangelist

John Mark, the traditional author of this gospel, at least from the time of Papias, a bishop in Asia around A.D. 130, is a person well-known in the Acts of the Apostles (12:12, 25; 13:5, 13; 15:37, 39) and the letters of Paul (Col 4:10; Philemon 24; cf. 2 Tim 4:11) and Peter (1 Peter 5:13). His close association with apostolic testimony in the person of the leaders of the early church is indicated in these verses. Both his home and family connections (Acts 1:13, 14) played an important part in these formative years of Christian history.

Leaving Jerusalem Mark spent some time with Paul and his team (Acts 13:5). With the decision to leave the mission as it moved across Asia (Acts 13:13) relations with Paul were broken off, not without some bitter feelings (Acts 15:39). The result was that Barnabas, out of loyalty to his cousin Mark, separated from Paul and went off with Mark independently to Cyprus.

Some years later Mark was restored to Paul's favor (Col 4:10), maybe at the time of Paul's imprisonment in Rome (a tradition reflected in 2 Tim 4:11). John Mark's presence in Rome is attested by his link with Peter, if 1 Peter 5:13 is correctly understood as referring to the imperial city.

Later church tradition brought Mark to Alexandria in Egypt where he died; and at a much later period his memory was removed to Venice where he became the patron saint under the figure of a winged lion.

The Setting of the Gospel

Mark's presence in Rome has suggested to a number of scholars his work as both Peter's interpreter (prior to the apostle's martyrdom in about A.D. 65) and as an evangelist. It is natural therefore to see this gospel as reflecting conditions in the capital city prior to the outbreak of Nero's persecution, which in turn followed the great fire of Rome in A.D. 64. The simplest way of looking at the gospel's life-setting is to see it as a deposit of Peter's teaching, recorded after his death and stressing the cost of discipleship, as that price had already been paid in recent events by the martyrs of the Roman church. Irenaeus, bishop in Gaul, wrote: "After their deaths (Peter's, Paul's) Mark, the disciple and interpreter of Peter, himself also handed down to us in writing the things which Peter had proclaimed."

The New Look on Mark's Gospel

The combined forces of literary criticism, the failure of the liberal "quest of the historical Jesus," and a new appreciation of the role of our gospel-writers as theologians in their own right have effectively demolished this simplistic understanding of Mark's gospel. What has come to occupy scholarly attention, however, is an array of competing suggestions to do with Mark's composition, place of origin, and purpose in writing. Some agreed results of recent study are found, however. These may be listed:

(1) Mark has collected a body of isolated paragraphs (*pericopes*), and he was the first person we know to have published them in connected sequence to form a narrative of Jesus' life. (2) The title of "gospel" (1:1) for his book is also his own creation, and he has done this to put into written form the oral proclamation of the "good news" the apostles preached. His links are far more with Paul than with Peter. (3) The story of Jesus' passion occupies a disproportionate amount of space for a special reason. Mark wants to emphasize the "theology of the cross," partly as an encouragement to martyrs in his day, but chiefly to show how central Jesus' death is in the church's ministry, liturgy and service. Mark composed his gospel "backwards," Willi Marxsen's dictum runs (see his work listed in the bibliography, p. 149). (4) Mark is much more than a historian offering a biography of Jesus, though an interest in Jesus as a human being is present, possibly to counteract a false idea that Jesus was not truly human (see 1 John 4:2, 3).

Why did Mark write? That question has been considerably broadened in recent study. "What sort of person in what sort of primitive Christian group would have been motivated to produce this sort of writing?" is how Howard Clark Kee asks it (see his work in the bibliography, p. 76). Answers fall under three main headings:

(1) *Apologetic interest.* Mark is believed to have a concern for his fellow Christians in Syria or Rome who were puzzled over the political events preceding the Jewish war of A.D. 66 – 70. He wrote to offer a philosophy of history to sustain their faith.

(2) *Pastoral Motives.* The inner life of Mark's church was, in this view, rent by faction and dispute, and was faced by a variety of a pressing pastoral needs caused mainly by the tension of Jewish believers who clung to their association with the earthly family of Jesus and his first disciples. Mark opposes this misplaced confidence (see E. Trocme's book listed in the bibliography).

(3) *Christological Disputes.* Most promising is the appreciation of Mark's gospel as a proclamation of Jesus Christ in narrative form. We are to think of his gospel refuting false notions of a Davidic Messiah or stressing Jesus' person as truly human, set over against the idea that he was a "divine man" or a hellenistic magician. His full share in our human life even to death repels the idea of a phantom-like figure cherished by some Christian groups, called gnostics. Above all the picture of Jesus as obedient son of God and suffering servant provides a model for authentic Christian living in terms of self-denial and sacrifice (8:34 –37). The last-named is perhaps nearest the truth, and we are best encouraged to read this gospel as a transcript in story form of Paul's teaching of "dying to live" with Christ, stated in 2 Cor 4:7 –12.

Setting the Stage
(Mark 1:1–8)

Mark's Title Page (1:1)

The page of a modern book that first catches our interest is the title page. We want to know what the book is all about. Ancient books had no dust covers or words printed on the spine to arrest attention. So the first page—or even, as here in Mark 1:1, the first sentence—had to convey the writer's main message. This is exactly what Mark's opening verse is trying to do: to alert the reader to what is to follow. It is both his "table of contents" and title page brought together in a bold statement.

(1) He calls his book, "the beginning," perhaps in a conscious recall of Genesis 1:1. If so, he is putting in a bid to gain our attention by asserting that a new start in the world's history is being narrated. God is at work in the coming and activity of his son Jesus Christ—and this should be a time of rejoicing as at the first creation and the world's new day (Job 38:7).

"Life is made up of new beginnings," said Alexander Whyte, the Scottish preacher. This is true because God is always starting something fresh—in history, in his church, in human lives. Mark 1:1 can be linked with Gen 1:1; and themes such as "God's new work," "Life's new beginnings," "A fresh start—with God" are suggested as sermon topics.

Mark's own biography could be used in illustration. We trace it in Acts 13:5, 13; 15:36–41 (his going back from the work) and in Col 4:10 (Paul's commendation of him) and in 2 Tim 4:11 (the tradition of his value to Paul). The overall theme is "Failure is not Final."

The life-story of John Mark divides into four parts. These may be our sermon skeleton: (1) "going back"; (2) "giving in" to remorse; (3) "starting over"; (4) "making good," not least in Mark's writing this gospel book.

(2) Mark's book proclaims good news (or gospel). This term had associations with the Roman emperor whose en-

thronement was regarded as "good news (gospel) for the
world"; with second Isaiah's announcement of a new age
when God would be king over the world (Isa 52:7–10); and
with the people of the Dead Sea scrolls who greeted the arrival of a new order of community life in the desert as they were
made ready by the cleansing of the Spirit.

You can relate these three ideas to the modern scene
where "good news" is in short supply! There's plenty of "bad
news" on the political scene, the economic front, or at the social level. But only because God is left out. Where he starts to
work, the outlook is transformed. Thus Mark's gospel and ours
too center on: (a) a new Lord of human lives and society (see
Acts 17:7); (b) a belief that God's throne rules over all the
world's confusion, and his purposes are secure; and (c) a new
society—the church—where men and women are cleansed
and renewed and equipped, not in a monastic community but
in the rough and tumble of life in the world.

(3) The story-line of Mark's gospel is that the time of God's
purpose to save the world has come in the bursting on to the
scene of Jesus Christ his son (1:15). Mark picks up the first
Christian creed—see Acts 8:37 (see *RSV* margin), 9:20; Rom
1:3, 4—and boldly asserts, Jesus is God's son. You can trace
this designation of Jesus running through his chapters like a
thread (1:1, 11; 3:11; 8:38: 9:7; 12:6; 13:32; 14:61; 15:39). The
three most interesting scenes are (a) at Jesus' baptism (1:11);
(b) at the transfiguration (9:7); and (c) at the cross (15:39). The
episodes are linked with Jesus' obedience, his decision to face
the cross, and his humiliation unto death. These three "win-
dows" permit us to glimpse what "Son of God" means.

A sermon on "The Sonship of Jesus" can focus on these
three "moments" in his life. They can be related to "His
Sonship—and Ours" with exhortations to follow Jesus in (a)
an obedience and service, (b) a readiness to suffer (you can recall Bonhoeffer's choice to leave the USA and return to his native Germany then under growing ominous Nazi power), and
(c) a willingness even to give our all ("When Christ calls a man
[or woman], he bids him come and die"—Bonhoeffer).

A sermon on "creedal religion" could pick up these items
in verse 1. Use the "fish" symbol (Greek *ichthus* = "Jesus
Christ is the son of God, the savior") as a lead-in; the text will

have three parts: (1) Jesus is God's agent, the anointed; (2) he is his son; (3) salvation is the start of a new day in personal and world history.

The Messenger in the Wilderness (1:2–8)

True, Jesus bursts on to the stage without an elaborate build-up. Mark passes over his birth and boyhood and has no apparent interest in his parents or background. Mary his mother is mentioned only indirectly (6:3), though we do learn from Mark that Jesus worked as a carpenter at Nazareth. He is the only evangelist to tell us precisely that.

The one person who does "prepare the way" is John. He sets people's expectation astir with his announcement that a great one, a more-than-a-prophet, a bearer of the Holy Spirit, is soon to be seen. John plays the role of Elijah, both in dress and diet in the desert (see 2 Kings 1:8) and, for Jews, well-versed in the OT the next person to come after Elijah's return would be God (see Mal 4:5; Mark 9:9–13).

"Preparing the way of the Lord" is a title obviously related to the Advent season. John's mission in life was (a) to be the messenger promised in Malachi and (b) to recall Israel to its national origins in "the wilderness" (see Hos 2:14–23), a place of divine revelation in Jewish thought. (c) John took his cue evidently from the hope of a faithful "prophet" who would appear in the last days (see Deut 18:15–19) and announce God's will for the nations.

Notice the ways John fulfilled and yet also disappointed current expectations. He raised human hopes that soon God would appear to inaugurate a new age; then he resolutely called for "repentance" (= a return to Israel's God) as a necessary preparation for that experience of the "good time coming." Sermons on "John the prophet" may conveniently focus on his role as a man who (a) announced the coming of God's messiah; (b) denounced the failures of Israel, especially the nation's leaders, to be God's true people; and (c) pronounced divine judgment, always with the promise of God's mercy and forgiveness to those who would act on his word.

The fate of John is postponed until Mark 6:14–29, though it is darkly hinted as in 1:14 (translate: "After John had been handed over. . ."). John's person and message were an unwelcome challenge to his contemporaries. He not only introduced the new age; he embodied it and so he rebuked the easygoing life of the nation's leaders. And he suffered for it. The price of his courageous witness can be seen in the link between 1:14, 6:14–29 and 9:12—three parts of his biography that may be joined in a sermon on "John's Role in History."

Jesus Appears on the Scene
(Mark 1:9–15)

Jesus' Baptism (1:9–11)

There are three parts to this opening cameo: (1) Jesus' baptism; (2) His testing; (3) His preaching. First, Jesus is baptized, an event both historical and symbolical. The outward circumstance is well-known as, at the hands of John called the "baptizer" (1:4), Jesus consents to a ritual washing as a sign of a new phase of his earthly ministry. Henceforth he will leave behind his private life as a village artisan, and embark on his public work as God's appointed agent for the coming of the kingdom which he both announced and exemplified (1:15). The "inner" meaning of this happening needs exploring in any sermon on Jesus' baptism, avoiding the trap of a psychologizing treatment as though we had secret access today to Jesus' life and inner thought. The most we can hope for is to ask what Mark's readers would have made of this story and try to answer that question.

The sky is split open, as a sign of God's "coming down" (Isa 64:1; Ps 144:5) to visit men and women. The Spirit, who had brooded over the old creation in the beginning (Gen 1:2), descends in dove-like form. The Father's voice echoes, at least in Jesus' hearing according to Mark: "You are my dear and only son. I have just set my favor on you." Augustine had the insight to see a picture of the Godhead here: "Go to the Jordan and you will find the Trinity." Here is a theme for Trinity Sunday suggested by: (a) the calling of the Father; (b) the consecrating of the Son and (c) the commissioning of the Spirit. Clearly the baptism marked a turning point in Jesus' earthly life, and these themes can be applied to a Christian's initiation to the church at baptism or confirmation.

The attentive reader of Mark would recall the OT motifs in 1:11. There is God's promise to crown the messianic son (originally Israel's king) as son (Ps 2:6–7). There is equally Yahweh's intention to commission his servant by his spirit to carry out his purpose in the world (Isa 42:1). If the reader dug a little deeper, he might see the parallel between Jesus the beloved son of the Father and Isaac whom Abraham dearly loved (Gen 22:2) and whose obedience to the patriarch's desires were such that he was willing to die. Jewish rabbis had an elaborate theory about the "binding of Isaac" as a merit-conferring act applicable to later generations of Jews.

Here is a cluster of images, all proclaiming "who Jesus is." A short series of sermons may be offered under that caption—don't attempt to cover the ground in one sermon! Subtitles would be: (a) He is *God's son* who is destined to reign in the divine kingdom. But the road to triumph and coronation runs by way of the cross. So (b) he is Isaiah's *suffering servant*, endowed with the Spirit as the Lord's anointed one (Acts 10:38). Above all (c) he is the *filial redeemer*, ready to offer his life in willing devotion to God's purpose because he loves God's will above all else. Mark will make this "obedience unto death" the high-point of his drama (10:45).

Jesus Is Tempted (1:12–13)

The better word is "tested" but in Lent congregations expect to hear about the "Temptations of Jesus." Notice that Mark compresses the episode into a crisp statement, using profusely the continuing imagery of the OT. The Jews were tested "in the wilderness" (Ps 95:7–11; Heb 3:7–19) and "forty days" reminds us of Moses on the mountain (Ex 24:18) and Elijah's sojourn en route to Mount Horeb (1 Kings 19:8, 15). Interestingly, both OT characters reappear in Mark 9:4, 5 which, in my view, is another temptation story.

No details of Jesus' time of testing are given, apart from the detail of the wild beasts (like Adam in Gen 2:19, 20) and the ministering of angels. There is nothing akin to the wealth of description given in Matt 4:1–11; Luke 4:1–13.

The reason seems to be that for Mark Jesus' testings extended through the entire course of his ministry. He is repeatedly "put on the spot" in his encounter with demonic forces (3:20–29) and in his debates with Jewish leaders (8:11–13; 10:2–9). So U. W. Mauser's conclusion (*Christ in the Wilderness* [London: SCM Press, 1963] p. 100) is warranted: "the whole Gospel [of Mark] is an explanation of how Jesus was tempted."

The temptations of Jesus all focus on his obedience to God's calling. Using the material from Matthew and Luke as illustration, we can see the three areas in which Jesus was tested. Always the question is uppermost, Will he stay true to his mission as God's agent and servant? F. W. Dillistone (*Jesus Christ and his Cross* [London/Philadelphia: Lutterworth/Westminister Press, 1953] pp. 22–25) provides us with three matching titles. Here again a series of three sermons is called for, rather than one gigantic effort to cover all the ground in a single attempt. The points of testing for Jesus were: (1) *The Snare of the Short Cut* by turning stones into bread and so pandering to man's appetites. Jesus could have won the world on a slogan of "No More Hunger," given the economic pressures on men and women in Israel in his day. The offer of utopia where all physical needs are met would have been irresistible. All men want bread; but there is no guarantee that any person wants to hear and live by the word of God. (2) *Playing to the Gallery*. The love of appreciation by our fellows and peers is deep-set. But to gain the applause by sensational means, by a gimmick or circus trick in the temple court, is not God's way. Jesus "would die rather than make a convenience or a cheap advertisement of the power and providence of God" (Dillistone). And he did. (3) *Forcing the Issue* involves the opportunity to hitch the kingdom of God to Satan's war chariot and to bring in God's rule by forcible, military means. Once more Jesus sets his face against the Zealot option and refuses the role of a warrior messiah, which was a current expectation.

So Moses and the manna, the apocalyptic razzle-dazzle to stun the crowds, the patriotic call to arms to set the nation free from oppression—all these were viable options set before Jesus in the wilderness. He rejected each one in turn, and resolutely set his face to doing the Father's will even if it meant the road to the cross. Observe that each of these ideas has its good points and powerful attraction and that Jesus, as truly human, must have been drawn to each of these ways to promote God's kingdom. The issue is not, is it good, but, is it best? A sermon title on "The Good—The Enemy of the Best" can use this setting.

The Ministry Begins (1:14–15)

The opening words of Jesus' preaching set the stage for all that is to follow. John's arrest and delivery to his fate are the signal to Jesus that his own destiny is about to be realized in a way not unlike that which befell John (see 14:21). At all events he knows the right time has come. A sermon on "Jesus' first words" gives a good opportunity to stress the interfacing of indicative (stating what is) and imperative (calling on people to act). The second depends on the first, whether it is in terms of invitation ("The meal is ready"—indicative; "Come and get it"—imperative) or warning ("The building is on fire. Jump through the window").

So Jesus' first announcement is a declaration. The critical hour has struck and God's moment in history, his *kairos*, is here. The sign is the presence of the rule of God which is already touching human lives in Jesus' person and ministry (see Luke 11:20). Now, in the light of these realities, repent or turn back to God, and put your trust in the good news. The last item is a gracious summons to do something. Later on Jesus will call on people "to enter the kingdom."

Christian preaching needs to keep this intimate connection between "fact" and "act"; either one without the other is incomplete and leads to a distortion of the role of the preacher. We have our calling to announce the good news of God's loving presence in the history of Jesus Christ then and now, and to point to all he has done. But we must then go on to summon our hearers to act, to respond, to live in the light of this truth, and "rise up" to follow Jesus in daily living and social concern. We shall see how this happened in our next sections of Mark.

A sermon outline on 1:14, 15 could include: (1) the right time, emphasizing that God is never in haste; (2) the good news, explaining how "gospel" is just that; (3) the direct call, inviting a response.

Jesus in Action
(Mark 1:16–39)

Mark the evangelist has just amazed his readers with his introduction of Jesus whose way is prepared by John who in turn does what Malachi the prophet (3:1; 4:5) had promised; and a new age is announced as "at hand" (Mark 1:15). We are taken "behind the scenes" to a "heavenly world" from which a bird descends and a voice speaks. The dove is a symbol of the Spirit's activity which had long been dormant in Israel; the voice is the Father's, announcing that Jesus is none other than his only son whom he loves. And finally Jesus opens his mouth to announce that God's rule, long expected and much needed in a time when the Jewish people smarted under the yoke of foreign oppression, is ready to appear. The question is bound to be raised, what will Jesus do first? In our passage we see him at work in three ways, and all of them contribute to Mark's understanding of what is meant by "the gospel."

Jesus Calls Helpers (1:16–20)

"Come, follow me" is the call addressed to the four men as they worked at their fishing trade by the Lake of Galilee. The language is familiar to us, but in its first context it is striking. It resonates with Elijah's summons and challenge to Israel on Mount Carmel: "If Yahweh is God, follow him!" (1 Kings 18:21), and if so, Jesus' authority is in evidence. He acts in such a way that men and women heard in his call the summons of God himself. This claim he is making, however tacitly, will soon land him in trouble (see 2:7, 3:6).

Mark tells the story of the call of the first four disciples in a way that emphasizes the radical nature of discipleship. Simon and Andrew leave behind their nets, symbols of their profession (see v. 18); James and John leave their father, their parental connection (see v. 20).

The call of the fishermen looks forward to the way Jesus will gather a company around him (3:13–19) and then send them out to be his agents (6:7–13, 30). So it is clear that Jesus is no solo performer, intending to do the work of the kingdom on his own. He is looking for associates who will share his company and be his representatives, both in the Galilean ministry and later when he has to leave them (14:28; 16:7). In the meanwhile Jesus will make them useful as "fishers of men"— a metaphor that goes back to Jer 16:16 but here used of "catching" men out of the turbulent waters of the world in the net of the company of Christ that expects God's coming reign (Anderson).

Note how, at the outset, the mission of Jesus involved his enlisting others to share the work with him: "Jesus, No Solo Performer" might convey this thought in a sermon title. And, as we shall see, his favorite title "Son of man" (found 14 times in this gospel) probably is used of Jesus in association with his disciples who became also his colleagues.

"Follow me" is a text we can use in a service of discipleship. Explain how relationship to Christ is (1) personal; (2) life-transforming; yet (3) societal, beckoning us to join Christ's people whose motto is service for others ("fishers of men").

Jesus' Mastery of Evil Forces (1:21–34)

He began to teach with firsthand authority (1:21, 22), not like the religious leaders of the synagogue who based their teaching on previous decisions taken by other rabbis and quoted precedents in support. Jesus never quoted the "authorities"; he taught with authority which he claimed as God's special agent for the bringing in of the new age.

To speak is one thing; to do something is another. Both in this story and again in 2:1–12 the issue turns on whether Jesus just "talks" or can perform. His effective response is to assert and prove that he does both. You might want to illustrate this from Acts 3:1–10 where the apostles both speak to the lame man at the temple gate and offer him a hand of help to lift him to his feet. "Matching the Action of the Gospel to the Word of the Gospel" is Leslie Cooke's appropriate way of linking the two sides of the church's ministry today.

Jesus' encounter with "demons" here at the Capernaum synagogue and later in a general setting (1:32) poses one of the hardest hermeneutical problems for the preacher. Notice that Mark apparently distinguished between sick folk and those demon-possessed (1:34). We today do not make such a fine distinction between physical and mental illness, though many people would prefer to keep an open mind as to the reality and power of "demonic forces," i.e., non-human evil present in society and human life. Some kind of demythologizing is necessary, though there is no denying the pervasive influence of evil forces that work to destroy the best in life. C. S. Lewis in the original preface to his *Screwtape Letters* (1942) spoke some wise words:

> There are two equal and opposite errors into which our race can fall about the devils. One is to disbelieve in their existence. The other is to believe, and to feel an excessive and unhealthy interest in them. . . . They themselves are equally pleased by both errors.

The gospels are more concerned to proclaim Jesus' victory over demonic powers than to speculate about evil; and in this story once again Jesus' authority is re-asserted, whether the enemies are the violent antagonism raised by the demoniac or the debilitating weakness caused by Simon's mother-in-law's fever. Jesus is seen as master of every situation, and all that would rob human life of its fullness and dignity yields to his touch. The "demons" in today's world could be spelled out in a sermon which "takes off" from Jesus' ministry of exorcism, as James S. Stewart does in a classic sermon, based on 1 Peter 3:19 ("He preached to the spirits in prison"). The imprisoning forces of human life are identified as (a) the fact of drudgery; (b) the pressure of the world; (c) the tyranny of sin; (d) the fear of death. And the sermon ends on the triumphant note: Thanks be to God who gives us the victory (see Stewart's volume, *The Strong Name* [Edinburgh: T. and T. Clark, 1940] pp. 24–34).

Jesus Met Temptation (1:35–39)

Peter and others track down Jesus as he had sought a quiet place for prayer. Observe again the logic of James Stewart's comment in *The Life and Teaching of Jesus Christ* (Nashville: Abingdon Press) p. 98: "the praying Christ is the supreme argument for prayer," for it is his example of fellowship with God for which he found it needful to retire momentarily from life's pressures that encourages us to do the same.

Just as remarkable in a different way is the news, "Every-

one is searching for you" (v. 37). Jesus was strangely indiffer-
ent to this announcement of his popularity and wanted to
move on. Modern scholars have shown how the verb "to seek"
in Mark's Gospel carries a bad sense, either with a plainly hostile reference to Jesus' enemies who want to kill him (11:18;
12:12; 14:1, 11, 55) or with regard to trying to distract Jesus
from his true mission (3:32; 8:11). Peter here as often is the
mouthpiece of the temptation, and it looks as though his inter-
ruption of Jesus at prayer was part of a satanic ploy (as in
8:33) to get Jesus to tone down his preaching of the kingdom
and stay in one settled place. A good sermon may emerge here
on "Misguided Advice," using Peter's naive remark as a way
in which to please the crowds at the cost of disobeying his
Father's call.

The Opposition Grows
(Mark 1:40—3:6)

This is a lengthy section devoted to a single theme in Mark's infrastructure. Recent scholarship has concentrated on "Jesus and his Adversaries" (see A. J. Hultgren's title given in the bibliography) by examining these "stories of conflict" and pinpointing the nature of the opposition which Jesus' ministry aroused. We can itemize the leading issues that formed the basis of growing controversy between Jesus and his followers on one side and the representatives of official Judaism on the other.

(a) Jesus claimed to forgive sins (2:5) in his word to the paralyzed man. This drew out the murmured comment: Why does this man talk like this? Who can forgive sins except God?

(b) He deliberately chose the company of tax collectors and "sinners" (2:13–17). The reason for bracketing these two groups will need to be explained to a modern congregation, even if the IRS officials are nobody's friends! Tax officers like Matthew and Zaccheus were Jews hired by the occupying Roman administration to collect several kinds of tolls, dues and sales taxes. But they were despised and cast out by the Pharisees because they had compromised their religious beliefs in Israel as God's land and their fellow-Jews as God's chosen people. They were beyond the pale of "true religion."

When Jesus reached out to these men he was making trouble for himself and quickly found himself having to justify his conduct. He answers simply: these persons are in need and I have come to meet men and women at their own level to raise them up. The "righteous" Pharisees lack this sense of need and so cannot appreciate what Jesus is doing. They prefer their closed system of rules and guidelines to Jesus' openness to human beings where they find themselves (as the later story in 7:1–13 will illustrate).

(c) Fasting was an important part of Jewish religious observance. It prepared, they believed, for the coming of the kingdom of God. Jesus took a casual attitude to fasting because he knew that God's rule had already begun. And that rule was more like a feast, making everyone happy. But not all can see that and when he is criticized for allowing his disciples such laxity he realizes that he is in the presence of his enemies. "The time will come when the bridegroom will *be taken away*"—the verb echoes Isaiah 53:8 of the suffering servant whose life is "taken from the earth." Jesus' mission and official Judaism are evidently set on a collision course.

(d) Of all the venerable institutions that were prized by the Jewish religion of Jesus' day none could rival the sabbath whose observance was treated with the utmost respect and seriousness. "Keep the day holy" was a commandment elevated to top rank. The question was hotly debated, however: what is permitted on the holy day? And what is "work"? Reaping and threshing were in the schedule of "work," so the actions of Jesus' disciples in the cornfields were in plain violation. Jesus countered the criticism with a simple assertion: the claims of his ministry in which God's rule is at work override even the time-honored laws of Moses as the scribes understood and enforced them. Again, these were fighting words, bound to stir up trouble.

(e) Jesus above all else was concerned with individuals— such as the man with the atrophied hand—as persons in their own right and so with a claim to respect and dignity which no institution or custom or religious ordinance, however respected or ancient, should deny. Again, there is hostility and a verse (3:6) points unmistakably to the way the future will be shaped. The prospects for Jesus' continuing fame and freedom are none too good.

Sermons on these themes, so vital in our understanding of who Jesus was and why he fell foul of his contemporaries, need to begin with the background and move deftly to show how Jesus challenges social conventions, ethical mores and societal structures today. Why should Jesus cause offence? We are in good company in posing the question for it seems that this was why the stories were preserved in the first place. It was because Jesus' popularity as a healer and helper could hardly explain why he made so many enemies and finished up on a cross. Christians needed to know what went wrong. These "controversy stories" are designed to supply the answer.

Basically the issue is between organized religion and the freedom of the Spirit. There have to be rules and guidelines in society and church; the danger comes when they are fossilized and hardened into dogmas and a cast-iron system that crushes people in the process. Even good customs can become fixed and inflexible, and it is a short step to the judgmental spirit that opposed Jesus and encompassed his death.

He came with a new teaching (1:27) of God's kingdom where there is joy like a wedding feast and liberty in the Father's presence to live as his children. Legalism would keep us in bondage, perhaps to the past and certainly to our prejudices and fears, whereas Jesus comes to set us free to be responsible, mature adults.

"Justification by faith" as acceptance by God and of one another may be preached from these stories, and the picture of Jesus as idol-breaker and "the one who disappoints" men's hopes is clear. John Baillie's prayer-thought that Jesus did not say, "You shall know the rules and by them you shall be bound," but "you shall know the truth, and the truth shall set you free" (John 8:32) neatly sums up the deep-down cleavage that lies at the heart of these conflict stories.

A topical sermon on any one of these "conflict stories" will be helpful. For example, on 2:1–12 you can analyze the various characters in the drama: (1) the needy man whom official religion couldn't reach; (2) the enterprising friends, determined to get the sick man to Jesus; (3) the authority of Jesus, both to heal and forgive; (4) the religious leaders with their concern for their "rules." They were interested not in people but in problems about people.

Three Groups Around Jesus
(Mark 3:7–35)

We can identify three sets of people who have contact with Jesus in this passage. Three sermons might usefully bring them together since they are a diverse cross-section of society and represent different parts of the populace. Yet all are associated with him.

(a) *The crowds*. They are often in the background of Mark's story and the evangelist uses them to point up Jesus' initial popularity and appeal. They represent human life at its most obvious need: oppressed by a wide range of fears, fickle in their swift change of attitude once their hopes of Jesus' kingdom-preaching are disillusioned. Yet they are responsive to his call in a way that puts both the official Jewish leadership and the disciples to shame. Men like the father of the sick child (in 9:14–27) and the beggar Bartimaeus (10:46–52) and women such as the foreigner of Tyre (7:24–30) are remarkable examples of "faith where you would least expect to find it." Mark holds these people up as shining witnesses to Jesus' power to enlist ordinary people. And they are here in 3:7–12.

(b) *The disciples*. Their call and names are given in detail (3:13–19). The point to remember is that everyone of them belonged to the class of society called "the people of the land" despised and disowned by the professional scribes and leaders. There is not a "religious" man among them. More than one of them seems to have had some link with Jewish nationalists called the Zealots, the freedom fighters of the Jewish resistance to Roman rule. Certainly Simon the Canaanean (Luke more correctly calls him "the Zealot") and possibly Judas and James and his brother John (Boanerges—sons of tumult) belonged at one time to this group. At the other extreme stands Matthew, the former tax superintendent now called from his office desk (2:13, 14). A good and valid point can be made of this surprising association. Former Zealots and an ex-compromiser and traitor to his nation's cause can come together in the new society that Jesus created.

Judas may well have been the only non-Galilean in the

bunch, if Iscariot means "man of Kerioth," a village in Judah (Joshua 15:25). Whether this fact, if true, would account for his treachery is doubtful and Judas remains an enigma, though congregations seem to show an inordinate curiosity over what made him tick and why he betrayed his Lord. The gospels do not help much to meet this question and leave Judas as a stark warning against half-hearted discipleship. Certainly his motivation includes more than love of money and there is no suggestion he was a coward out to save his own neck by turning "state's evidence." A sermon on Judas should not fail to include: (i) Jesus' well-intentioned call of him as a potential recruit. It is monstrous to think otherwise. (ii) Jesus' continued appeal to Judas, as in the tender scenes of John 13:21–30. (iii) Jesus' warning that "one of the Twelve" will betray him—and so by extension a caution to all professed followers that mere "associating with Jesus" is not enough unless we really share his spirit and live by his standards. (iv) Notice too that the unmasking of Judas took everyone except Judas by surprise; "Lord, is it I?" they all said. That's a healthy attitude, and there is no room for a judgmental verdict on this man.

"Judas" as a sermon theme has to be handled with care lest we say too much on the basis of little data. Perhaps (1) the enigma of Judas or (2) the example of Judas is as far as we can safely go. See the present writer's article on "Judas," *The Illustrated Bible Dictionary* (Wheaton: Tyndale House, 1980) vol. 2, pp. 830–31 for details.

(c) *The family.* Scarcely less puzzling is the hostility and misunderstanding created among Jesus' own kinsfolk, including his mother. The verse which introduces them (3:21) should probably be read: "his family went to take control of him, for they said that he was mad"—not a very flattering estimate of those nearest to Jesus in blood relationship! Jesus' rebuff of his family which follows (3:31–35) lines up with what we have said. For him earthly relationship is on a different level from a spiritual union, and with E. Trocmé *(The Formation of the Gospel According to Mark* [Philadelphia: Westminster Press, 1975] pp. 131–36) we may suspect that Mark's own antipathy to James and the entire family of Jesus in the later church is reflected. This suspicion grows stronger when we read the story in 6:1–6.

Whatever the cause, Mark does not shirk from recording one of the severest words of Jesus in the gospels. He warns of "the blasphemy against the Holy Spirit." Again, a homiletical nettle has to be courageously grasped by any preacher venturing into this territory. As a first essential, one must make clear that in its historical context the charge that occasioned the warning was that Jesus is "possessed by Beelzebul" (3:22) when he casts out evil spirits. The implication is that he is in cahoots with the devil and that's why he is so successful. Jesus appeals to logic. If I am in league with Satan, as you say, why do I spend time in trying to destroy Satan's work and setting his prisoners free? How can Jesus and Satan be partners when each tries to outdo the other?

"Blasphemy" in this sense is a complete confusion of moral values and issues. It leads to the notion that Jesus is aided and abetted by the devil and is, in fact, doing the devil's work for him. He is no better than Satan's Messiah; and to claim that is to be so morally confused that "forgiveness" has no meaning since the person involved doesn't know the difference between right and wrong. He is saying, in effect, like Milton's Satan (in *Paradise Lost*): "Evil, be thou my good." So his sin, while he is in this state, remains. Many folk are genuinely puzzled and upset over "the sin that never has forgiveness," so an alert pastor will address this pastoral problem with the preceding paragraph in mind. Persons who are worried about their sins may be assured that their very concern is a sign that they can be forgiven.

Jesus the Open-Air Preacher
(Mark 4:1–34)

    With a new method of operation—Jesus began to preach in the open air as the door of the Jewish synagogue closed against him—there came a new style of public speaking. He taught the crowds in parables, we read (4:2).

    The parables of Jesus are a favorite seed plot for many a preacher's sermons; but they are tricky! So often we resort to allegorizing the details or using the stories as pegs on which to hang ethical homilies. These aberrations are not new, and the history of interpretation reveals some amazing curiosities regarding the way the parables have been treated in the past. But that is no excuse for us in our day.

    Parables are vivid observations of nature and human nature. They speak of everyday, commonplace things, events, situations and problems. Jesus tells a story, in the first place, to gain the hearer's attention and to enlist his sympathy. Then, his parables bid us take a further step. This is to consider the best in life as a hint of and then a stepping-stone to an awareness of what God is like. Finally, they set a bench-mark by which we can measure what we ought to be and how we should respond to God's rule present in Jesus. So they are invariably "parables of the kingdom." In the light of what happened when Jesus came with the news of the Father's rule, the parable, says T. W. Manson, "shows us what kind of God we must believe in and what kind of persons we must be" *(The Beginning of the Gospel* [London: Cambridge University Press, 1950] p. 41).

    One further point to grasp. Throughout this type of teaching Jesus has his eye on false ideas about God's reign and wrong-headed notions about the way that the kingdom comes into human experience. The parables are not just pretty tales to tickle our fancy or to entertain us. Nor are they embroidery to clothe moral principles such as all people accept. The parables offer the ethics of life in God's kingdom and they launch counterattacks on current wrong ideas about God, his purpose and life under his rule. They are his "weapons of war-

fare," as J. Jeremias called them (*The Parables of Jesus*
[Philadelphia: Westminster Press, 1963] p. 19) by which Satan's realm is invaded and his house robbed (see 3:27).

Let's take *three selections* from Mark's collection which
represent evidently a grouping by the evangelist of this genre
of the Lord's teaching.

(a) The story of *the sower* (4:1–20) is as much about the
seed and the different soils. But the title is well-named, for
this piece of farmer's lore centers on the effectiveness of Jesus'
own teaching. In a sense, it is a parable about the other parables. The key term is "word" (Greek *logos*) found eight times
in vv. 13–20.

The sower sows good seed in every place. In some places
the harvest is lost, but that is not the fault of the seed. When
the seed does enter "good ground" there is an amazingly pro-
ductive harvest far greater than any Palestinian farmer would
imagine. This is the token of the new age Jesus has announced
and which the Jews were expecting. Talk of fecundity and harvest bounty would appeal to Jesus' hearers who would recall
Amos 9:13–15.

At another level Mark's own readers would want the reas-
surance in this parable that *their* efforts would in the end be
crowned with success. Despite wastage, failure due to human
unresponsiveness and satanic countermeasures the effort is
worthwhile; the "secret of the kingdom" (v. 11) is to be shared
among a great number. Perhaps the sombre warnings of v. 12
are meant to encourage faint-hearted preachers, struggling to
be faithful in time of persecution and falling away, that the
work is God's.

(b) That encouragement is certainly the theme of the next
little vignette: *the seed growing secretly* (4:26–29), a parable
found only in this gospel. The lesson is one of patience, which
is the trademark of the farmer (see James 5:7). He buries the
seed in the earth and awaits the harvest. There is nothing
more he can do once he has sowed and awaits the time of reaping. The message is clear. God will take care of his kingdom in
his own way. There is no need for his people to be anxious, or
to try to hasten its coming, as the nationalist Zealots were doing by their guerilla campaign against Rome. Let preachers
be assured that once with Paul and Apollos they have planted

and watered it is God who alone can make the seed to germi-
nate and grow (1 Cor 3:6, 7).

(c) The third parable in the series is the story of the *mustard seed* (4:30–32). It is the graphic account of small beginnings that produce a magnificent result. The tall tree, sprung
from a speck of seed, gives hospitality to "the birds of the air,"
a biblical phrase (Ezek 17:23; 31:6; Dan 4:11,12, 21) for the
Gentile nations. So God's kingdom begins small but grows
large. Planted on Jewish soil, it will soon spread out its
branches until it offers shelter to the nations. Again, no reader
of Mark's words could miss the hopeful significance of Jesus'
ministry that began in the relative obscurity of the Galilean
countryside but in Mark's day was already making a bid to
capture the center of the empire for God.

Preaching from the parables presents a great opportunity. The vital thing is to seize on the story's central point and
back it home with illustration and repetition. The sower,
seeds and soil will leave our hearers in no doubt as to their responsibility to hear and obey and be fruitful. The seed that
grows without human effort corrects any imbalance and reminds us that human responsibility is only part of the matter:
God is sovereign. "Rise up, O men of God," even without its
sexist tones, is only half the truth.

> Sit down, O men of God,
> His kingdom He will bring,
> Whenever it may please His will;
> You cannot do a thing

is just as unnecessary a caricature as the well-known hymn.
We need some equipoise between God's sovereignty and control and our part in responding and working for the kingdom.
"Expect great things from God: attempt great things for God"
is the phrase to capture the truth in both extremes.

The mustard seed story is a marvelous missionary text,
reminding our congregations not to despise the day of small
things, and to be ready to promote the expansion of the rule of
God by all means at our disposal.

A sermon outline on 4:26–29 could be: (1) divine sovereignty, since it is God's kingdom and he is in charge; (2) our
responsibility, since the farmer must till the ground and sow

the seed; (3) united action, since both are needed to produce a
harvest. Without God we cannot labor; without us God will
not work.

You can approach these parables indirectly as well. With
a caption like "Ideas Jesus Rejected" you can indicate how
mistaken notions of the gospel message are exposed and refut-
ed in these stories. The enemies are (1) indifference and neg-
lect; (2) impatience; and (3) scepticism, corresponding to the
three parables. But be sure to end on positive notes. Finally,
remember that our hearers as in Jesus' and Mark's day have
so many half-baked ideas about what God is doing in the
world that they need patient instruction in a language and idi-
om as relevant and down-to-earth as Jesus' stories in
parables. Kierkegaard the Danish philosopher said: "Wrong-
headed ideas are like a cramp in the foot. The best cure is to
stamp on them."

A Cluster of Miracle Stories
(Mark 4:35—5:43)

Mark has joined together a "complex" of four miracle stories to demonstrate Jesus' power over nature and human nature, climaxing in his victory over man's last enemy. There is an impressive build-up. Evidently the theme is: What God did long ago Jesus is doing today. Here is a lead-in to a sermon series on "The Contemporary Christ."

Lord of the Wind and Sea (4:35–41)

The sea of Galilee lies in a basin, and is subject to storms caused by a sudden change in atmospheric pressure. On this occasion there was a great storm of wind, of gale force, which quickly had the small boat in danger (4:37).

Jesus was asleep in the stern—a detail only in Mark (4:38) who wants wherever he can to stress the humanity of Jesus. He was tired out at the end of the day. But his sleep was a picture of perfect trust in the sustaining and protecting care of God, as often in the OT (Ps 4:8; Prov 3:23, 24; Job 11:18, 19; Lev 26:6). So it is the example of Jesus as the man of faith, the model believer that this story portarys. We can take a sermonic cue here: "Jesus as Faith's Example."

The disciples, on the other hand, are full of fear and petulance, turning on Jesus who is suspected of negligence: "Teacher, are we to perish, for all you care?" But he is the master of the situation and in words which only this gospel records as direct speech he speaks to the waves as to a turbulent spirit, "Peace! Be still!" literally, "be muzzled," 4:39. All is quiet.

The OT background here is vital. One of the great attributes of Yahweh is that he controls the sea and subdues the chaos-monster, Tehom (akin to the Babylonian Tiamat, overcome by the hero Marduk). Tehom is rendered sometimes "the deep," referring to the ocean which the Jewish people feared. See Ps 89:9, 10; 93:3, 4; 106:8, 9; Isa 51:9, 10, and especially Ps 107:23–30, a drama very similar to our story.

In Mark the punch-line is "Do you not yet have faith?" (v. 40). This is not asked for information but to express surprise on Jesus' part that his men are still unbelieving. This experience should convince them that he is none other than the Son of God, God's presence and power in a human life, since he does what Yahweh did long ago in stilling the sea. Not surprisingly the disciples are filled with "fear" (v. 41), i.e., reverence and awe as they ask, "Who then is this?"

The final question might be our text, with answers drawn from this episode. Jesue is both truly man and truly more-than-human, God in human form, *Deus praesens*. And he is *God-with-us*, since there is evidence that church fathers like Tertullian saw a parable here. The "little ship" of the church is often rocked in the storm and nearly swamped unitl the Lord of history comes to his persecuted people, as in Mark's church, and rebukes the oppressor. Sermons on "With Christ in the boat" or "Faith driving out Fear" are suggested from this incident. The wording of v. 38 is the same as in 1 Peter 5:7, "He cares for you," but with obvious differences. Here is material for a two-part sermon on "The Caring Lord" challenged and affirmed. Or use three ideas (1) our cares as a source of trouble; (2) his "care" for us; (3) "leave your worries with him" (1 Pet 5:7, Good News Bible).

The Exorcist (5:1–20)

This title for Jesus was locked away in scholars' testbooks until recently. Now, since the publication of William Blatty's novel and the movie based on it, it is a word on many people's lips. If you use the story-line of *The Exorcist* as an introduction, it is worth a comment that both book and film miss the really significant point. Both are unhealthy exploitations of a serious theme, especially with their gruesome scenes and sordid details, justifying the *Los Angeles Times'* review that this is a movie for "strong stomachs and weak minds."

The essential point, obviously missing from much modern discussion of exorcism, is Jesus' victory over demonic forces. In this story once more (as in 1:21–27; see comments there on demons), Jesus is presented in total command of the scene, and knows exactly how to deal with the menacing approach of this demented man. The popular belief was that if the name of the demon could be known, its evil power was overcome (v. 9).

Mark's story has many aspects. On the surface he wants to show the contrast between the man in his manic depressive state (vv. 2 –6) and the change that came over him once he had met Jesus and been set free (v. 15). But the story as we have it seems to have gone through several editions and its final form is that of a missionary challegne, seen in vv. 19 –20.

Our expositions should therefore stay with the main thrust of the episode and not get sidetracked into questions about the 2,000 pigs. If you do want to say something about them, we all know pigs are unclean animals for Jews, which suggests that this story took place on Gentile territory in northeastern Galilee where there was a strong pagan population. More to be observed is the typological significance of the pigs' destruction, intended to prove that the power which held the Gentiles captive was itself destroyed, as in 1 Kings 18:40.

The story for us has two motifs: (1) Jesus' power over evil that cannot be glossed over or dealt with easily. The man offers resistance as Jesus comes near: "Don't torment me" (v. 7). This is a good starting point for a sermon whose theme could be "The Disturbing Christ." As he "interferes" (v. 7) with our lives, we find it painful and call on him to keep his hands off. But his wounds are for our ultimate healing just as a surgeon has to "injure" as if be is to get at the root cause:

> Beneath the bleeding hands we feel
> The sharp compassion of the healer's art,
> Resolving the enigma of the fever chart,
>   (T. S. Eliot, *Four Quartets*)

(2) Jesus' mission was one of "Making People Whole," perhaps another sermon title. If so, we can go on to the end of the story and show how the new life this man received led him to want to serve others. I suggest a simple outline, one (it seems) that might appeal to most congregations who like to be able to carry away at least the "headings" of our discourses:

(1) The refusal of his request (v. 19);
(2) The sphere of his service (v. 19);
(3) The theme of his testimony (v. 20).

A Woman's Faith (5:25–34)

One of the interesting features of Mark's literary style is (his) "sandwich" structure, that is, a running together of two stories laid one on top of the other. The account of the sick woman is layered into the other story of Jairus' daughter.

The first story is full of human interest which deserves a dramatic re-telling in any sermon based on it. The "point" of the tale, it would appear, is the distinction the storyteller makes between two types of physical contact: there is "thronging" (v. 31) as the crowds jostle and press on Jesus, pushing and rubbing his shoulders, and there is "touching" which is what the woman intended to do (v. 28) and which Jesus immediately recognized as more than mere physical proximity (v. 30). The disciples, as often in Mark's Gospel, are at a loss to know the difference (v. 31).

But it is a vital difference. The crowd has contact with Jesus accidentally; the woman comes near to him with a set purpose, and she is rewarded in a special way. They were in a carnival mood, out for some excitement and curious to see a spectacular miracle in Jairus' home. The woman had a need as she came to touch Jesus as a last resort and a final hope. That's the way she came to him.

She got from him that day all she could ask for, and then some. Her bonus blessing was that she had a word personally addressed to her (v. 34)—and that would be her passport into society once more. As a "woman of uncleanness" (see Lev 15:25–27) she was ceremonially unclean and a social outcast. Now she gets an entree back into both society and synagogue. She expected to be cured and to slip back into the anonymity of the faceless crowd she had left. Instead, she is singled out and given a personalized miracle all to herself.

Any of the above sidelights of this story can be worked into a sermon. The most obvious is the contrast of two types of contact with Christ: some are only spectators at worship, while those who meet him face-to-face gain real help. Nor should we despise a very naive "faith" like the woman's in v. 28. It looked more like superstition to want to touch his clothes—except that Jesus recognized it as living faith (v. 34) and pronounced her "saved" (so the Greek: recall that salvation and health go together: God's purpose is to make us whole persons, which is what "being saved" is all about). "Go in peace" (v. 34) could be a text, starting from what *shalom* means; and the woman gained (i) wholeness as a person; (ii) a new life in society; and (iii) a new outlook on life.

Victory over Death (5:35–43)

Death is still the number one issue in many people's minds and secret fears. A century ago sex was a taboo subject and hushed up in polite conversation, while preparing for death was part of life's business. Now the order is reversed; but death still haunts us if secretly and we all have a hidden phobia. If a man die, shall he live again? remains a big question.

The central thrust of the Christian message is that death has no power to hurt us. Death's reality and its solemn significance are not denied—how could they be?—but "the sting of death" as Paul calls it has been drawn and neutralized. This confidence is based on Jesus' own resurrection, but also on his power to call us from death to life. Hence this story was cherished in the church, especially in time of persecution when the threat of death's imminence was real, as in Mark's church.

Jesus calls death by the tender word, "sleep" (v. 39): not to deny that she was dead but to promise that he had come to awaken her. He does this with a word (preserved in his native Aramaic) as natural as a mother's morning call to a drowsy infant, "Little one, it's time to get up" (v. 41). Paul learned too that death is like a sleep (1 Thess 4:13–15; 5:10; 1 Cor 15:6, 51) and that the resurrection is a fundamental Christian belief, in spite of appearances to the contrary.

A sermon on "Death's Defeat" from this pericope could start from the crowd's reaction (v. 40): they jeered at him. They knew she *was* dead. Probably it reflects a natural disappointment at being kept at arm's length and so excluded from the sick room. Jesus was no wonder worker, out to enhance his reputation with a sideshow of miracle-working. This explains no doubt his caution to keep the miracle under wraps (v. 43), though it is hard to see how his order could be followed. After all, there was one extra person who came out of the room! Perhaps the "messianic secret" relates to the way he raised up the girl lest it should lead to a wave of popular superstition that would impede his real mission.

Jairus' faith is called into play, and it must have needed a strong confidence to take Jesus at his word. "Do not be afraid. Only believe" suggests a text ready-made for encouraging Christians to persevere. The Greek verbs mean: "Give up your fear; Keep on believing," a nice distinction worth exploiting.

Above all, Jesus appears as Lord of every situation, even when it is seemingly hopeless. Be sure to go on to say that we who live on the other side of Easter have more to bolster our faith than ever Jairus did. "Because I live, you will live also" (John 14:19) is the basis of our faith. People laughed at Jesus (5:40); now because of Jesus and his victory at Easter, Christians laugh at death (1 Cor 15:54–57).

Jairus' daughter and her recovery give us the opportunity to preach on (1) Jesus' compassion; (2) Jesus' encouragement; (3) Jesus' practical concern (v. 43).

Martyrdom and Misunderstanding
(Mark 6:1 –46)

John the Martyr (6:14 –29)

John the Baptist has already been on the stage as the "prophesied preparer" of Jesus' way, a role drawn from the OT (Mal 3:1; Isa 40:3; Ex 23:20). Yet not everyone was pleased with John's other messages, especially when he came near to bone and exposed the sensitive nerve-endings of King Herod's love life. He boldly denounced the way Herod was playing around in high society and Herod's wife-swapping practice (6:17–18) merited his rebuke.

Herod was an ambivalent character, who couldn't make up his mind about John. He both respected and hated him; but he imprisoned him to silence his voice nevertheless.

Herodias, Herod's mistress, however, had no scruples at all. Her attitude was strictly personal and selfish, and she was determined to safeguard her own position as Herod's spouse, even if the Jewish law did not allow it. She knew that John's caustic warning was correct, based on Lev 18:16; 20:21; but also that "the only place where her marriage certificate could safely be written was on the back of the death warrant of John" (T. W. Manson *The Servant Messiah* [London: Cambridge University Press, 1953] p. 40).

So her ploy is explained, involving her daughter at Herod's birthday celebration (vv. 21–28). The sequel is well-known and can be told from the pulpit with dramatic force. A review of the story will pick up various motivations: John's courage, Herod's vacillation, Herodias' malice, the daughter Salome's complicity ("The picture of a Herodian princess dancing before such an audience is outrageous," comments Hugh Anderson). Nor should we overlook the disciples of the Baptist (v. 29) who claim their master's headless corpse and bury it (Matt 14:12 adds, "and went and told Jesus"). They prefigure the other disciples who bury Jesus' body (15:42 –47) but they did so with only John's memory to remain with

them. On the subject of John's disciples (Matt 14:12) I once
tried to picture their needs in a sermon: (1) in *loneliness* it was
their greatest privilege to go and seek Jesus; (2) in their *sorrow*
it was their surest comfort to go and tell him; (3) in their *per-
plexity* it was their highest wisdom to bring their doubts to
him.

Jesus evidently saw in the fate of John a foreshadowing of
his own destiny, though Jesus' end will lead to a different outcome. If Jesus is called to a martyr's fate, he will reappear to
guide his people as the risen Lord. Two sections of Mark also
prepare the reader for the tragic ending of Jesus' earthly life;
both are based on misunderstandings.

Rejection at Nazareth (6:1–6)

"Local Boy Makes Good" might be the headline to greet
Jesus' visit to Nazareth, his native village. He has already
picked up something of a reputation as a wonderworker and
teacher, and his effectiveness can't be denied. But the people
at Nazareth are puzzled about him. After all, he is only the village carpenter turned preacher (v. 3: note this is the only place
on record where Jesus is called "the carpenter"; elsewhere he
is the "carpenter's son" which is not the same thing).

He worked with his hands, a point Mark likes to emphasize in other ways. The "hands of Jesus" play a significant role
in this gospel, specially to do with healing (1:31; 5:41; 6:2;
7:33; 8:23, 25; 9:27; 10:16) and if you are pressed, you can fit a
suitable adjective to the noun and get a series of addresses on
"The Hands of Jesus" as compassionate, tender, powerful, etc.
Laying hands on people is not as common in the contemporary literature as one might expect and is not evidenced before a
recent discovery of the Dead Sea scroll library (the *Genesis
Apocryphon*). Christians evidently took special interest in this
act and saw it as a mark of close identification. So Jesus' acts
were performed by hands (6:2) that were (1) strong (in cleansing the Temple); (2) gracious (to receive children in 10:16); (3)
wounded at Calvary; (4) yet victorious after death (Luke
24:50, 51).

> The hands of Christ/Seem very frail,
> For they were broken/By a nail.
> But only they/Reach heaven at last.
> Whom these frail broken hands/Hold fast.

The incident at Nazareth raises some nice exegetical questions, chiefly to do with the attitude of the local people whose hostility is not disguised at all ("they took offense at him," treating him as a scandal—the Greek word is *skandalon*, a rock over which a traveller stumbles). Why?

Answers could provide sermon outlines, as follows: (i) At least one reason for the frosty reception Jesus received in his hometown was *his humble origin*. People were scandalized that a working-man should do works of power that claimed God's kingdom had come in his person and presence. The claim was more than they could take, since current expectation was largely centered on a warrior Messiah or a glorious figure whom God would reveal at the end-time. So they refused Jesus who seemed to be just an "ordinary" prophet-preacher with no nimbus around his head and whose feet touched Palestinian soil at every point. Mark loves to accentuate the full humanity of the Lord. (ii) Calling him "Son of Mary" may suggest the same, but there is a specific nuance to this title. To address a man as the son of his mother was *a calculated insult*, suggesting that he was born to her while she was still unmarried. It is like our vulgar expletive, Bastard! This explanation is more likely than the traditional view that Joseph, Jesus' putative father, was already dead and so his mother's name is included. A second reason for his being rejected is the insinuation that no true prophet could have such a dubious parentage. (iii) Above all, it was *lack of faith* that caused even Jesus to be shocked (the verb in v. 6 is a strong one: "he was astounded at their unbelief"; the only other occurrence when used of Jesus is in Matt 8:10-Luke 7:9 where Jesus is amazed at the centurion's faith, a nice coupling of two opposites). We are in touch here with Jesus' genuine reaction: in the very place where he may have expected a sympathetic response the attitude is hostile, as though to underscore the point that earthly attachment to Jesus avails little unless it calls out our trust at an existential level. The extent of this unbelief is seen by his inability to do any (messianic) works at Nazarath; his hands were tied and he could not—a daring assertion of something he *could not* do—reveal his true person.

The Feeding of the Crowd (6:30–46)

The Twelve have been sent out on a mission and have returned. If we place in parallel columns the account in Luke

10:17–20 which reports the success the apostles had scored in
their preaching and healing tour, we can see how disturbed
Jesus was at their elation. Flushed with success, they were beginning to prepare for the immediate appearing of a glorious
kingdom that Jesus would usher in. Their hopes were again
raised when, after a period of retreat where no doubt Jesus
tried to teach them other lessons, everyone was faced with an
acute problem. There were 5,000 persons on hand who needed
something to eat at the end of a long day.

The temptations of Jesus in the desert, only glanced at
in Mark but described in Matthew and Luke, pinpoint the issue. Would Jesus turn stones into bread and create a new
utopia of plenty? Would he stun the people into belief by
playing the part of Moses and the manna? Evidently the disciples, fresh from their success, were laying plans for a messianic uprising once Jesus had declared himself; otherwise
who are "the many" who keep coming and going? And why
do they hurry to meet Jesus in v. 33, which suggests a wide-
spread, premeditated and united movement, intent on
crowning him as king?

Jesus faced this crowd with mixed feelings. On the one
hand he felt compassion and concern (6:34), but equally he
sensed the danger of a mob that was ready to stampede into a
violent uprising against Roman power. "As sheep without a
shepherd" (v. 34) suggests to us a congregation without a pastor, but the metaphor, drawn from the OT, refers to a
leaderless crowd of men like an army without a general (Num
27:17; 1 Kings 22:17)—a danger to themselves and everybody
else. And especially at Passover time (Mark notes the "green
grass," a condition true only in Galilee in the early spring-
time) when Messiah's appearing was expected.

So Jesus acts in a symbolic manner. The crowd is to sit
down in what appears a military formation (vv. 39–40) but
there is now a surprising twist to the story. Instead of a mirac-
ulous provision of messianic "bread from heaven" Jesus sets
the example with a single family's rations—five bread rolls
and two sardines—and shares these meager supplies with
others. What happened next is anybody's guess. Did this supply become "eucharistic" (as John 6 interprets the incident)
and meet the spiritual needs of the crowd? Did Jesus' example
set a trend so that those who had brought food started to share

with others? Or did the "loaves and fish" miraculously become multiplied under Jesus' hand?

Whatever it was, it was enough to set the people's imagination working overtime and the Fourth Gospel correctly
notes the effect: they wanted to come by force and make Jesus
king (John 6:15). But he fled from this suggestion and with-
drew to the hills as an escape from their abortive enthusiasm.

"The Day Jesus Ran Away" based on the story-ending
may focus a sermon on the reasons for his abhorrence of becoming king "on a bread basis," as G. Campbell Morgan once
called it. This miracle story certainly claims the preacher's attention because it is the only miracle story to appear in all
four gospels and it is the most dramatic of the synoptic mira-
cles. It also marks something of a turning point in Jesus' ministry, and it opens a window on the conflict he faced
throughout his public life. He was alive to the temptation that
was continually pressing upon him. It was the snare of the
shortcut (see earlier on 1:12 –13) when he was offered an easy
road to popularity and success.

He resisted the temptation when an easy path lay before
him. And he provided—in the most likely interpretation of the
incident—a better way to meeting human needs than pandering to a carnal desire to see wonders performed. Let every person share out of a concern for his neighbor's needs. Also we
should not fail to emphasize that what Jesus brings to our
world is not a quick solution to economic problems and social
distresses but a new spirit of selfless outreaching to others and
a desire to win the world's allegiance by service.

So he could not accept the crown on the basis of a reputation of a social benefactor and provider of free lunches. The
only crown that wins our authentic allegiance is the crown of
thorns.

Any sermon on the Feeding of the Crowd needs to include:
(1) Jesus' deep commitment to social needs (the crowds were
hungry); (2) Jesus'-desire to lift the sights of people to their
spiritual needs; (3) Jesus' self-giving (in John 6). There are (1)
social; (2) messianic; (3) eucharistic dimensions here.

What Went Wrong?
(Mark 6:47—8:26)

So far in Mark's story we see that Jesus has few friends who understand him. There is an excitable crowd who tag along to have their curiosity aroused and several groups of enemies. The most puzzling group are the disciples who think of their master as a wonder-worker and national leader who needed, above all else, a good public relations agency to promote his cause in Galilee. They can't believe how he let slip a marvelous opportunity to win the crowds at the "feeding of the 5,000." So they need yet another lesson. This comes in 6:47–52: the walking on the water.

Once more we have to read the story through insight from the OT. God announced his identity as I AM (Ex 3:14; 6:6), and Jesus follows suit (v. 50). So Mark's readers needed to be assured that in Jesus God is personally present—to quieten the storms of life and to minister to ordinary folk at the levels of their existence where they need the most practical help—in sickness and distress (6:53–56). What the disciples miss (6:52) is plain to these simple Galilean peasants, even if there is a lot of superstition and naive faith mixed up with a genuine appreciation of who Jesus is.

Now in several areas Jesus puts into practice his understanding of what his mission entails.

Defense Against Religious Fanatics (7:1–23)

The Pharisees reappear on the scene; we last met them as they plotted his downfall (3:6). Mark is concerned now to explain to his readers the reason for their opposition. There are two test cases. Indeed Pharisaism as a religious way of life could be summed up by these two items: ceremonial purity (7:1–4) and the sacredness of vows (7:10–13). Together with other interests these matters made the Pharisees a group devoted to the serious pursuit of the Jewish religion, based on "the tradition of the elders" (7:3). The phrase refers to a body of authoritative rules and procedures that had grown up alongside the Mosaic law and offered an explanatory commentary on it. It showed how the Torah was to be applied to real-life situations.

The question turns on God's requirement to have a holy people. What is holiness, and how can a person be "holy" in everyday living? The Pharisees gave clear answers, first to do with ritual purity. A person could get "defiled" in strict pharisaic eyes by contact with non-Jews; even the shadow of a Gentile falling across food or kitchen utensils made them "unclean." So these items needed to be kept "pure," or as the Jews say, "kosher".

We may applaud the intention of this way of looking at life; it is serious and disciplined. But it quickly can degenerate into fussiness over detail and an overly picky attitude to externals and minor matters, as Mark's list makes clear (vv. 3 – 4).

Jesus cut through this camouflage to the heart of true religion, which is the religion of the heart. He exposes this concern for the outward trappings which cloaked the importance of the inward disposition. The explanations later given (vv. 20 – 23) go to the root of the matter: a person's inner life, his or her motivation and secret thoughts are what determine character, not a busy attention to details that gives a false sense of what is important and so frowns on other people who don't do it like we do. A sermon on "The Inner Life" can show how Jesus' teaching is as up-to-date as the latest book on "pop psychology."

The second matter is more intricate. Vows could be made to withdraw money or property from ordinary use to "sacred" purposes, e.g., the work of the temple. But the owner still retained the title of possession, and could use the excuse of having "dedicated" the money (the word is *korban*, 7:11) to get himself free from responsibility. It was, as we say, a "cop-out" since the possessions were safe and secure for as long as the owner wished. Yet he was relieved from obligation—even when his parents in their old age (and there was no social security or welfare to help out) needed his support.

Jesus dealt with this situation for what it was: an evasion of the fundamental duty to "honor" one's parents in the name of "religion." So he lays down a clear principle: no religious custom or device, however laudable it seems, can overthrow the elemental duty of love. A sermon of this discussion will need to begin with the Jewish background (see the commentaries for details) and quickly move on to some modern examples of "The Duty of Love" or "Love that Obligates."

God's Unrestricted Love (7:24–37)

The uncleanness of kitchen wares is not the only kind of uncleanness the Jews abhorred. They extended this attitude to persons, especially those of other races. The woman in question has three disqualifications: she was a born loser on three counts: she was a woman (a sad misfortune, in the eyes of the rabbis, all males of course); she was a Greek, her national or ethnic status was wrong; and she is called "Syrophoenician," a racial term but having inevitable and unsavory connections with the bastardized religion of Tyre and Sidon ever since Jezebel's time. How could she win?

But she did. Not because she had three counts against her, but because she had "faith" and it worked (vv. 29–30). So we can enquire what that faith meant. Her approach was (a) altruistic as her daughter's needs brought her to Jesus; (b) persistent in refusing to be rebuffed by Jesus' strangely cool response; (c) and inventive as she launches into a repartee with him.

She reminds Jesus that, at mealtimes, at the moment when all attention is given to the children's needs, the dogs are permitted to eat whatever food falls as scraps on the floor. In other words, she sees that Jesus' coming is much bigger than a ministry to the Jews. She was a member of a race whom they called "Gentile dogs." She owns up to that fact, but skillfully turns it to her own advantage. Messiah surely has a bigger concern than for one race, just as even the dogs get some food. She is rewarded as Jesus praises her quick-witted argument which (apparently) has his objection answered! A sermon title on "When Jesus Met His Match" could explore the issues involved in this story which the early church must have found slightly embarrassing but it preserved it nevertheless.

The reason is deeper, however. In Mark's day it was clear that the gospel which began in Galilee had spread to the heart of the empire. So Mark has his own interest in the phrase, "Let the children *first* be satisfied" (v. 27), because "first" implies that "second" will be the mission to the Gentiles, as in Paul's

missionary program (Rom 1:16), "to the Jew first *and also* to
the Greek." Israel's Messiah who came to release the tongue of
the dumb (Isa 35:6 which has the only other occurrence in the
Greek Bible of Mark's word in 7:32) is indeed Lord of the nations. These two healing stories have a missionary thrust.

Jesus and His Credentials (8:1–13)

This section stands almost at the center of Mark's Gospel;
it is certainly, whether by intention or not, the turning-point
in Jesus' relationship to the religious leaders of his day. It
leads on to the confrontation with the disciples at Caesarea
Philippi in the following section and raises the momentous
question, who is Jesus and how did he think of his mission?

The prologue to the debate in 8:11–13 is a feeding of the
crowd that runs parallel to the earlier feeding story (6:35–
44). The setting is so close that many think we have a
"doublet" or carbon copy story that Mark has inserted.
While, however, there are many "look-alike" features in the
two stories, there are equally significant differences. Most
noticeably the number is 4,000, not 5,000; and there are
seven not five loaves available. More interestingly the locale
is non-Jewish, as indicated by the place-name (in v. 10). This
fact suggested to Augustine, back in the 5th century, that
the second account was designed to portray Jesus as the
bread of life to the Gentiles.

With such a pagan (or certainly non-Jewish) location as
the Decapolis region and the stress placed on the hunger of the
masses who had travelled "from a distance" (v. 3: a symbolic
allusion surely, as we see the moment we stop to ask, "far . . .
from where?" The best parallel is Ephesians 2:13, used of the
Gentiles who were "afar from God" before they were brought
near by the cross of Jesus). It seems clear that Mark wants to
emphasize once again the missionary outreach of Jesus. And
so he places the challenge of world mission before the church
of his day.

The "feeding" stories can therefore with some justification be used as missionary texts, and "Jesus as Bread of Life
for the World" is a suitable title. The eucharistic setting of the
narrative is prominent too (see the actions described in v. 6)
and there are links with the later church's supper meal, as we
see by reading 1 Cor 11:24 in tandem with our verses in Mark.

The link between "feeding" and "communing" was meant in
the first place to convey the thought of "fellowship" or "sharing." So sharing our material goods with the needy is a pre-
requisite to our participating in the sacrifice of Christ (see 1
Cor 10:16). The key-term is *koinonia*, fellowship, which became something of a technical term in the early church and
has some powerful lessons for us today—provided we are prepared to understand the word in its true setting.

The next pericope (8:11–13) is only short but packed with
dramatic and theological explosive. We are in the midst of the
ongoing struggle between Jesus and his enemies. The Pharisees arrive on the scene to start an argument. The issue turns
on whether he is really a prophet come from God. If he has indeed come from God, would he kindly oblige them in the way
that Moses laid down? Would he give them a sign from heaven
which, according to Deut 13:1–2 was the true prophet's
accreditation?

Jesus refused point-blank. The reason lies once again in
the motive behind the request. These men were, in the Markan
story, insincere and wanted only to trip Jesus up. Their asking
for a sign from God, i.e., some phenomenon that would unmistakably prove Jesus' claim, like handwriting in the sky, was a
temptation (v. 11). It was the old story of the devil's insinuation at the outset of Jesus' ministry, inviting him to jump
down from the temple ledge and float gently to a "three-
point" landing in the temple forecourt, upborne on the arms
of God's angels.

Jesus again disappointed these inquirers, for a reason
that is not far to seek. No amount of "proof" or demonstration
will convince a person who has already made up his mind to
resist the claims of fresh evidence. "My mind is made up.
Don't confuse me with facts" is the tacit response. Only God
can change his outlook. "Signs" will do no good. A person who
is determined to disbelieve will try to explain away the marvelous sign and say that it is done by magic or conjuring tricks
or that he has heard and seen other people do the same thing
(as in Matt 12:27; Luke 11:19, statements which recall
Pharaoh's magicians in the Exodus stories).

And it was the same attitude that Paul found. The Jews
look for signs, he sadly observes (1 Cor 1:18–30). But his response was of a different sort. We offer Christ on his cross (1

Cor 1:23) and we trust God to reveal his wisdom and power in
a message that is foolishness to the "man of the world," the
"natural man" (1 Cor 2:14). "God's Wisdom in Christ's Cross"
would be a fitting sermon title for this theme. And you could
"take off" from the modern playwright Joe Orton's comment
that the traditional letters INRI on the cross ("Jesus of Nazareth, king of the Jews" in Latin) meant for him no more than I
Now Represent Idiots. So speaks the modern contempt for
Jesus' claim which only God's wisdom can vindicate and
overcome.

Jesus came into collision with the leaders of the Jewish
church. In a sense it was inevitable, ever since Jesus began his
ministry of concern and compassion for the outcasts of Israel
and placed the demands of the kingdom as a top priority.
What *is* unexpected is the way the disciples cherished ideas
that brought them to the point of a woeful misunderstanding
of what their master really intended to be and do. They
seemed to be attracted to the very ideas that Jesus criticized
as the "leaven" (or false teaching, in 8:15) of the Pharisees;
and he had to give them a stern warning because they were so
dull and misguided (v. 17).

"Signs" as a sermon title will have three sides: (1) *false*
signs (8:11) such as bogus prophets today claim (TV evange-
lists, parading their "cures"); (2) *ambiguous* signs (in patriotic, civil religion; or charismatic claims to the Spirit's
fullness); (3) the *one true* sign (the cross on the hill: see 1 Cor
1:18–24).

The key to Jesus' attitude lies in his questions about the
loaves used to feed the crowds, and the broken pieces picked
up by the basketful. That action is symbolic. It looks forward
to the Upper Room meal when Jesus will take the bread and
break it as a token of his body (14:22) to be given over to death
for these men and indeed the Gentiles ("the many" of 10:45)
on the cross. That was his secret mission. For them it must
have seemed "Mission: Impossible" because they were ob-
sessed with worldly ideas and they were wrangling over petty
concerns (8:16).

So matters—the course of history in particular—have
moved to a show-down. Mark's artistry is never more clearly
seen than in what follows. A series of character study sermons
can usefully focus on the chief *dramatis personae:*

(a) *The crowds* misunderstand Jesus' purpose, and see him only as a wonder-worker or even a potential leader in their struggle to be free from Roman rule.

(b) *The disciples* are led astray by false notions and need to be warned of the "leaven of the Pharisees and Herod" (8:15).

(c) *These leaders*—the names Pharisees, Herodians, neatly summarize religious and political power blocs in Jesus' Galilee—are becoming increasingly and openly hostile, as Jesus refuses their challenge, since to meet it on their terms would be a betrayal of what he claimed for himself and how he understood his mission from God. They have no idea of what real faith is, for "faith ceases to be faith when it clamours for visible or tangible proof" (Hugh Anderson).

(d) Yet all is not total blackness. There is a ray of light and hope, even if it shines in unlikely places. Take the case of *the blind beggar* who comes for Jesus' healing touch (8:22–26). He is restored in two stages, by the application of a "Second Touch" (Keith Miller's title). At first, the man can distinguish objects but they are out of focus and blurred. Then he gets a sharp picture on his retina, as Jesus touched him again.

Some preachers will want to use their imagination here. "The Dangers of Short-Sightedness" can help some people to advance from seeing only a distorted picture of life into a full vision of total experience in fellowship with God. A traveler to South Africa caught a glimpse through a porthole of his cabin on Table Mountain with the first light of dawn on it. He called his wife to share a breath-taking sight; but she replied, "Look, how dirty the porthole is!" She saw men like walking trees.

Or else you can explore the ways Jesus is never satisfied with second best. He goes on working in human lives until the work of grace is complete.

But do begin with Mark's purpose. He intends us to see the point as it is applied to the Twelve, who are also blind. They see who Jesus is, but it is indistinct and hazy. After the cross, they will get new understanding, as Jesus appears in the light of his vindication (14:28; 16:7). And they will get a preview of this vision in the last part of the next scenario.

Confrontation, Challenge, Claims
(Mark 8:27 – 9:8)

Mark 8:31 – 38 contains a section that functions as a watershed. All that has gone before has been leading up to it. All that follows will flow from it. The incident at Caesarea Philippi stands at the center of the Gospel of Mark, at a midpoint of the chapters. It represents Jesus' furthest journey away from Jerusalem and Galilee. After this confrontation in the northeast part of Israel's territory and his transfiguration on the slopes of a nearby mountain, he turns southward. He is headed for Jerusalem en route to his passion and Easter victory. In 8:27 – 9:1 we are at the parting of the ways. Henceforward the shadow of his impending destiny to suffer and die will fall ever more deeply across Mark's story page. But it will also be tinged with light that promises final glory, of which the vision in 9:2 – 8 is a pledge and assurance.

There is a deeper reason for the centrality of this section than Mark's literary expertise. "Here begins really for the first time the gospel as it was later preached by the apostles." Julius Wellhausen's perception correctly noted how Mark's Gospel is dominated by Paul's gospel: both center on "the crucified Christ." That phrase is a genuine paradox, since it brings together two contradictory ideas. "Christ" stood for a title of honor and glorious majesty, as in the *Psalms of Solomon*, written in 50 BC in anticipation of Israel's triumph over her foes at the hands of a warrior prince whose crusade would liberate the nation and lift Jerusalem to an eminence for all the world to see. The prince's name is "God's Messiah" or chosen one. He is hailed as a conquering hero, flushed with success.

To imagine him as suffering in defeat is really unthinkable. But to predict that he would die a shameful death, such as the term "cross" implied, is to speak in nonsense language, like talking today about a "square circle." It's just not possible! This is the problem posed at Caesarea Philippi, and it explains why Jesus' strange words about suffering, rejection and death fell on the bewildered disciples' ears but never really sunk in. Hence the passion predictions are repeated later.

It equally accounts for Peter's violent reaction—most striking in Mark's account—and Jesus' repartee which is just as vigorous (v. 33). The stand-off between Jesus and Peter in this dramatic scene can make a powerful sermon theme, especially if we can flesh out the conversation with some explanatory comments, and sketch in the background.

I suggest the entire section falls into three parts (perhaps each can be handled homiletically separately, and you can get three sermons from these verses):

    (a) the question Jesus asked (vv. 27–31)
    (b) the destiny Jesus accepted (vv. 32–38)
    (c) the glory Jesus displayed (9:1–8).

(a) The disciples have been in Jesus' company for some time now. Already they have formed some impression of him and are no doubt wondering who he may be. So Jesus' question to them, "Who do men say that I am?" is not unexpected. There are rumors filling the air. He is thought to be a great leader of Israel such as John the Baptist or Elijah come back to life. But Jesus presses the issue: "Who do you say that I am?" Peter is both leader and spokesperson: "You are the Christ," the Messiah.

Notice how Jesus received this tribute with some indifference, and told the disciples to keep his messiahship under wraps (v. 30). Why? Clearly he was embarrassed by such a title, presumably because it was heavily politicized and nationalistic. It would have given exactly the wrong impression of what he claims for the kingdom of God. It would have inflamed the people and suggested notions of worldly success, political power and violent "messianic war."

Jesus firmly believed in the coming of the divine kingdom—but it would come only in God's way and at his time. At what point in his ministry he saw a terrifying vision of the way God's rule is set up and its method of operation we cannot say. But at Caesarea Philippi one thought seems to have mastered him. The road to his messianic glory runs by way of the cross. His title to lordship is in a life of service and obedience that will lead to his death.

"No cross, no crown" is a familiar theme, but we need to repeat it often. Sermons on God's reign should start and end with the cross; and you can play off Peter and Jesus who both had their own ideas of kingly power, but they meant something quite different by it. Peter speaks of victory through might; Jesus will achieve his triumph in obedience and sacrifice.

(b) Jesus' favorite self-description is "Son of man," a title whose antecedents go back to Dan 7. There it stands for a remnant of faithful Jews who, in the Maccabean times of Syrian oppression and persecution, stood firm and were vindicated and owned by God, and then received an empire (Dan 7:22, 27). But they won through only because they first endured suffering and hardship (Dan 7:21, 25, 26). This seems, amid the scholarly debate over the Son of man title, the most likely meaning Jesus gave to his use of the enigmatic words. He thought of himself as one chosen by God to suffer and yet to be brought by God out of defeat to triumph. Then God's kingdom would come.

If we take our cue from Dan 7, another side to "Son of man" comes into view. The term stands for a representative figure who brings with him a company of people, just as a shepherd needs a flock of sheep or a king rules over a country. The title speaks of a group. In this case, it is Jesus plus the Twelve. If Jesus is bound to suffer before the kingdom comes, the disciples are involved in it with him.

That was bad news for them. Peter voices his disgust over Messiah having to be defeated and even to die. "Messiah," as we saw, suggests a glorious figure. So he cannot understand everything that he hears Jesus say; yet what he does understand, he doesn't like. Suffering will affect him and the other men in the group, and from that prospect he recoils. You could illustrate by a frank comment made by a girl who was asked, in a radio talk-show, which figure in history she would like to have been. "Joan of Arc," she replied, "but of course I wouldn't want to be burnt at the stake!"

The dialogue between Jesus and Peter is full of drama. The two disputants are at "cross" purposes, since at the heart of the discussion is the cross. "Get behind me, Satan" (8:33),

spoken to Peter, is a bold rejection of Peter's mistaken idea of a
political or revolutionary Messiah. Jesus faced the grim reality of his future suffering, but not blindly as though he had no
choice except to accept a cruel, irrational sentence of doom.
Though the cross was evil in itself, he will gladly accept it as
the Father's good will, since out of it will come the best of all
results, the arrival of God's kingdom. And he looks forward to
his vindication (v. 31).

The haunting question remains from v. 34 on: will Jesus
go to Jerusalem and to his death alone? Use the idea of a cor-
porate "Son of man" to indicate how discipleship entails loyalty to the suffering Christ. To be a loyal follower of Jesus, the
disciple must be ready to take his place in the "Son of man"
and be faithful even if it means death. Paul's teaching on "dying to live" (in 2 Cor 4) is germane here, and can be brought in
illustratively (for instance, "I die every day," 1 Cor 15:31 or "I
am crucified with Christ . . . [yet] I live," Gal 2:20).

Sermons on "Discipleship," "Counting the Cost" and
"Taking up the Cross" are suggested here. There is a volunta-
ristic principle in "taking up the cross" (v. 34) since what is in
mind is acceptance of hardship as (1) a personal choice; it is
not something forced on us and (2) it is for Christ's sake, out of
loyalty to him; it is not an accidental circumstance of life,
common to all.

People today need these two reminders, since they naturally think of "cross bearing" as a picture of some inconve-
nience or picayune trial, like a touch of arthritic pain or
having to work for a grouchy boss. These can be frustrating
and bothersome, and it is natural for us to say, "It's my cross.
I'll have to bear it."

But that's *not* what Jesus or Mark had in mind. This
"cross" business was no metaphor, since anybody in first-
century Palestine was only too well aware of the "cross," having seen what the Romans could do to slaves and social mis-
fits on the roadsides. For Jesus to promise that being his
followers meant "taking up" a cross would be horrific. As C.
H. Dodd remarked, "To carry the cross . . . that is the picture
which the words of Jesus conjured up in the minds of those
who heard him. They were to go to Jerusalem like a proces-
sion of condemned criminals with halters round their necks"
(*The Founder of Christianity* [New York: Macmillan, 1970] pp.
94-95).

Sermons on "bearing the cross" have to begin here. True discipleship, as J. Schmid defines it from Mark 8:34 (*The Gospel According to Mark* [Cork: Mercier Press, 1968] p. 154) is not only "Follow me," but "Die with me." But dying is a prelude to new life, so the Christian can claim as his or her theme-song, "God forbid that I should glory save in the cross" (Gal 6:14, KJV). A suggested outline might be: (1) Wearing the cross, as a talisman or fetish. Inadequate ideas could be exposed. (2) Bearing the cross, as the hallmark of authentic discipleship. (3) Glorying in the cross, as we look ahead to final vindication (8:38).

(c) Jesus spoke about the glory that one day would be his—and theirs, if they were faithful to the end (8:38). The question remains: what of the immediate future? Are there encouragements to give strength for the trials ahead for the disciples?

There are two such prospects. First, there is the promise of Jesus himself (9:1) that some of the present company would not die until they had seen their faith rewarded. In historical terms they would live on to Pentecost when Jesus' resurrection and exaltation to the Father released the new age of the Spirit, the "kingdom of God come with power" (so Calvin). The second support lay only a week ahead. Then, on a spur of Mount Hermon in the company of the favored three disciples Jesus underwent a metamorphosis (the Greek word in 9:2: "he was transformed in front of them"). Here was a pre-vision of his final glory, in a visible and dramatic way, spoken of earlier at 8:38.

The key to this strange narrative, akin to Greek stories of divine theophanies in which the gods make appearances, lies in the appearance of Elijah and Moses (v. 4). Peter wants to erect three tents or booths for the three chief actors as though to capture these moments forever and never let the three leaders of Israel, representing the law, the prophets and the new age, go. Most commentators argue for this meaning.

There may be a deeper sense, arising from the use of "booths" which suggests a celebration of the Jewish festival of Tabernacles (based on Lev 23:39–43). Even today in Israel, in the fall of the year, pious Jews relive the experience of their ancestors throughout their desert wanderings and build shaded patios in which at least one meal a day is taken during Sukkoth, the festival of Booths. It has always been a time of

intense nationalism and patriotic fervor. I suggest that Peter
is trading on this fact. By offering to build three booths, he is
calling on Jesus to lead the nation to freedom (as Moses did)
and to put down all their enemies (as Elijah did). Moreover,
these two men never died in the ordinary way; both "died"
mysteriously and in triumph. Is Peter in effect saying to Jesus,
"Step up to glory from the mountain, like your predecessors—
and take us with you to your kingdom"? If so, he is again rebuked (v. 6) and has no answer to give.

When the cloud comes and obscures them, the disciples
are left wondering. But as it clears and the Jewish leaders of
old are nowhere to be seen, it becomes clear. Jesus is still
with them (v. 8). He has not gone into heaven. Instead the
heavenly voice identifies him once again (see 1:11) as God's
special son, whom Moses spoke of (Deut 18:15) and calls him
yet once more to leave the mountain for the valley where
there is human need. That road down will lead to the cross.
So Jesus faced the issue not for the first time. The road to
glory is not upwards but downwards (as the same kinetic imagery of Phil 2:6–11 powerfully describes with his choice
and commitment to obedience much in prominence). The
way to receive the crown is to accept first the cross. The
"thoughts of men" (to go back to 8:33) are contrary to the
"thoughts of God," just as God's kingdom is not man's empire on a bigger scale.

> The Kingdoms of the Earth go by,
> In purple and in gold;
> They rise, they triumph, and they die,
> And all their tale is told.
>
> One Kingdom only is divine,
> One banner triumphs still.
> Its King a servant, and its sign
> A gibbet on a hill.
>
> (G. F. Bradby, *The Way;* Oxford: Oxford
> University Press, 1921)

The simplest of outlines is needed to convey these stark
choices. From the viewpoint of these "men of the mount"
you can trace their experience as (1) *seeing a vision*, true and
false; (2) *hearing a voice*, both confirming Jesus' own deci-

sion and rebuking their low desires for worldly success; (3) *making a venture*, in company with Jesus on the road down to the levels of human misery (9:14–27) and ultimately to the bitter cross.

Faith, Frustration, Failure
(Mark 9:9–50)

These three human experiences are graphically portrayed in several stories and pieces of teaching in our chapter. They can be illustrated from Mark's accounts. We will, however, deal with the chief contents of the unfolding drama of Jesus' life as the evangelist records it.

The Disciples' Frustration (9:9–10)

These men are genuinely puzzled. They have heard their teacher speak of a Son of man who is bound to suffer (8:31) before he receives the crown (8:38). They have just seen his splendor on the mountain and heard the heavenly voice booming out of the cloud (9:7), telling them that the prophet of Nazareth is greater than the greatest man of their ancestral religion, Moses. The two chief men of the OT retire and disappear, and their master is left alone in solitary splendor. All this is great. But there is a snag.

What disturbs them is that he goes on to talk of the Son of man's "rising from the dead." Is that Son of man first to die? It seems so, but how can that happen, when he is all the time a glorious figure (Dan 7:13) who is received at the throne of God and crowned with honor?

"Faith's Puzzle" could be a title for their dilemma, and it is resolved by Jesus' words in three statements (our sermon headings; and how could they be bettered?): (a) Daniel's Son of man gets to the throne only along the road of affliction as the faithful Maccabean Jews were ready to die for their faith. This is a thrilling segment of Jewish history, largely unknown to our congregations but worth retelling, using the location of Masada, the Israeli tourist attraction and the "Zealots' last stand" (Y. Yadin's subtitle to one of the best books on the period, *Masada: Herod's Fortress and the Zealots' Last Stand* (New York: Random House, 1966) as object-lesson. (b) The OT prophets talk of another figure whose vocation, given him by God, is to suffer on the people's behalf. This is the suffering servant of Isaiah 53. The language of Mark 9:12: he "must suffer much and be treated with contempt" recalls the fate of the servant. (c) And if the disciples had the wit to see it, Jesus' commitment to suffering has already been dramatized before their eyes. John's martyrdom has already occurred, implying that John is more than a forerunner. He has set the pattern of suffering for Jesus to follow. But Jesus is more than a martyr for a noble cause. His death alone will save the world because he is the "greater one" John foretold (Mark 1:7). Nonetheless John was not like Elijah who escaped the wrath of his enemies—herein is the "paradox of prophecy"; it is both fulfilled and yet in the process its mold is broken—but met his fate head-on. The Son of man can expect no less (9:12).

These three parts to a sermon on "Christ and his Destiny" or "The Disciples' Dilemma" will give you a chance to offer an expository treatment of a theme whose importance is central to the Christian faith. It touches on matters as fundamental as (a) the road to glory via suffering; (b) the "truth" of OT fulfillments which are not always to the letter but transcend the expectations; (c) Jesus and John: how they agreed and differed.

The paragraph (9:9–13) is a bit complicated, but worth a sermon with headings such as (1) the disciples' questioning; (2) Jesus' enigmatic reply; (3) the resolving of the mystery—in the cross. The point of the sermon is that there are no "easy" answers to life's mysteries; that Jesus sometimes mystifies rather than clarifies; and that in the end life's unsolved enigmas have to be viewed in light of the cross. This kind of sermon could be a corrective to the image of Jesus as "super problem-solver."

The Disciples' Failure (9:14–16, 28–50)

Attention switches to what has been going on during Jesus' absence with the three of the inner group. In the valley they had been presented with a problem and an opportunity, and they had blown it. The later verses simply continue their record of sad failure. You can itemize the different ways they came short of the standards Jesus expected of them:

(a) They failed to help the man whose son was demented because of their argumentative spirit (v. 14) which betrayed the more serious malaise of a lack of faith (vv. 16, 19) and discipline (vv. 28–29). The disciples admitted to their failure which was only too obvious. The sad word of the boy's father was "I asked your disciples to drive out the evil spirit, but they couldn't." Evidently they had tried and failed.

Their failure can be a starting point for several sermons on "Failure" whether we hear in this word the complaint of our society registering disappointment with the church, or the disciples' own confession of impotence. Perhaps we can be generous in remarking that at least they tried to help this man. But the reasons for their failure need to be faced squarely. The text speaks of three causes (lack of faith, of prayer, of discipline [= fasting]) which can be applied to the modern scene. Above all, Jesus' control of the situation brought fresh hope.

(b) They were still in doubt over Jesus' purpose. When he taught them plainly, and for the second time, that he came to die, they shake their heads in total and blank disbelief (vv. 30–32). And "they were afraid to ask him." Why? Nothing paralyzes faith like fear. . . and unnecessarily so.

(c) They still cherished ambitious plans for their own ego-building enterprises. So Jesus has to give them some lessons on the theme of greatness. The "visual aid" is a little child set in the middle of the group (v. 36) and lifted up in his arms (as in 10:16). Only the child-like spirit—one of lowliness, trustfulness, and simplicity—gets to understand God's kingdom.

(d) The Twelve compound their pride with an arrogance that wants to exclude others and despise them. So the man who practices exorcism and claimed to be engaged in the service of Jesus gets the cold-shoulder treatment because he didn't belong to their "group." Jesus warns these men of the danger of a narrow, sectarian spirit. "No Closed Shop in the Kingdom" is T. W. Manson's heading for verses 38–41 *(The Beginning of the Gospel* [London: Cambridge University Press, 1950]); and it could be our sermon title.

(e) One remaining peril is perhaps the most serious of all. They are in danger of leading other persons, especially the "weak" brother like the exorcist of v. 38, astray (v. 42). The punishment is fearful and is paralleled by what the Romans did to the Zealot freedom-fighters in AD 6 according to historians. Jesus used a well-known fact of Roman cruelty to point up a solemn lesson, warning against leading others astray by our careless example and selfish spirit.

Picture language is again in use in the references to

"Gehenna" (9:43). This was the valley of Hinnom, a ravine south of Jerusalem, which was used as the city trash disposal. The garbage was burned here and the place acquired a reputation as a place of destruction. So it becomes associated with the punishment of sinners in the future life and fire was the destructive element.

Jesus' warnings were meant to shake his hearers out of their complacency. They were thinking, "The Gentiles will burn in hell." Jesus turned it around, "You will suffer in an awful place like Gehenna if you live in a way that causes other people to stumble through your bad example." Notice how Jesus' most searching warnings were directed to two classes: the religious leaders of his day, who should have known better and given a truer example, and his own professed disciples who adopted such censorious ways that they denied in their conduct the new life he called them to exemplify. These "uncomfortable words" of Jesus were spoken whenever leaders of others placed stumbling blocks in the path of simple folk and tried to stop and thwart their entry into the kingdom of God. Sermons on "Hell" are just as needful today, provided we aim their thrust at the people who most need to hear them! Their function is not evangelistic in NT preaching, but as warnings to Christians, especially those who are lax and careless and, above all, judgmental of all and sundry.

Faith's Shining Example (9:19–27)

This story, found only in Mark, is one of intriguing interest, a masterpiece of Mark's storytelling ability, and with a punchline to make it memorable. I have used it in a sermon on faith, titled "Things you always wanted to know about faith, and were afraid to ask." More simply, it speaks of "Faith: its example, testing and reward."

The boy is sick and the father has an obvious need of help. But the nine disciples are confessedly powerless. Perhaps we should not judge them too harshly as this was a difficult case. The boy's complaint was long-standing, his symptoms distressing, and there was no apparent hope.

But there was one ray to brighten the gloomy scene. The father's cry was, "If you can do anything, have pity on us and help us" (v. 22). Jesus sees the glimmer of faith and picks up the father's phrase: "Did you say, 'If you can'? Why, everything can be done for anyone who has faith." The response is "I do have faith. Please help me in the little faith I have." And that attitude sets in motion a train of events leading to the boy's cure.

I suggest three lines of development in this vignette, all to do with faith.

(a) *The example of Jesus* comes through in the verse just quoted (v. 23). Normally we are quick to apply this tribute to the power of faith in reference to the Christian believer: if we believe, then all things are possible. I think that in its original setting it referred to Jesus, the man of faith who is claiming the confidence to see the boy healed on the ground that he trusts his heavenly Father to work through him. We get a fresh insight into Jesus' own life of trust here, and it calls us to share his faith in the limitless energy of God to touch and heal human lives.

(b) *The testing of faith,* however unpleasant, is a factor built into this story. The boy in fact is not immediately cured. There was a violent convulsion and he "became like one dead." Indeed, the murmured comment of the onlookers was, "He is dead" (v. 26), which means that in a terrifying moment, the father's trust was sorely tried and doubts began to rise: "I asked Jesus to cure my son, but look, he has killed him." "I am worse off now. I did have a living child, even if he was sick. Now the boy is dead." But such heart-rending fears are groundless. The boy is aroused and he stands upright, completely cured. But things had to get worse before they improved.

You can discuss here the way faith is no magic cure-all nor instantaneous success, turning all our difficulties into pleasures with a wave of the wand. Often faith leads us to a harder life, as Peter explains (1 Pet 1:6–9); and the only faith worth having is one that endures life's trials.

(c) *The discipline of faith* is taught in v. 29. Nothing comes easy, not even faith. Simple, naive fideism is a sham. Faith is God's gift, but it is not cheap. We have to exercise faith, cultivate it, live by it—and work at it (see Paul's paradox in 1 Thess 1:3: "your work of faith") to promote its growth by "prayer and fasting." The disciples failed at a crucial point, and modern disciples need the reminder: No gains without pains.

So this story illumines "faith" in its several facets and

forms. Even a "little" faith (v. 24) can work wonders, and the gospels agree that nothing so excited the spirit of Jesus as human faith in action:

> Faith, mighty faith, the promise sees,
> And looks to that alone;
> Laughs at impossibilities,
> And cries, it shall be done!

(Charles Wesley)

The Way of the Cross
(Mark 10:1–52)

The section that opens at 10:1 marks the onset of Jesus' journey south to Jerusalem on his final mission. It is parallel with Luke's so-called "Travel Section" (in Luke 9:51–18:14 or 19:44), though true to form, Mark's record is much shorter and with few models of Jesus' teaching. Mark's theological plan, however, is just as evident. Once Jesus has received the disciples' confession, however inadequate it may be, he began to teach them plainly about his sacrifice; and it is just as clear as in Luke that the sacrifice on the cross could only be made in Jerusalem. So the story moves with inexorable destiny from Galilee by way of the right bank of the Jordan river on to Judea—and Jerusalem.

What Mark lacks in precise geographical detail and recording of Jesus' teaching at length, he makes up for in vivid narrative and gripping word pictures. The most lifelike piece of writing in the entire gospel comes at 10:32. It is a scene worthy of the artist's canvas and brush, and the preacher's most dramatic style. Jesus and the Twelve are on the road to Jerusalem. Jesus is striding ahead of them, as though he wants to make all speed, while they strangely lag behind. They are amazed—presumably at his eagerness to march on Jerusalem, yet they follow him even if fear grips them. They are fearful, it seems, because of the uncertainty of the future ahead of them. He is courageous and confident because he knows that only in Jerusalem can the Father's will be worked out, even though it involves suffering and death (10:32–34). This scene would make a fine introduction to a Holy Week series in which Jesus' purpose and the disciples' fear are played off against each other. The motif of a "journey" can be used as an organizing theme, since it recurs in the phrase "on the road" in chapter 10. Alternatively we can select the central theme of the kingdom of God and see how it stands at the heart of the various pericopes in this chapter.

The Kingdom: Its Arrival (10:1–12)

As soon as he sets foot on Judean soil a fresh conflict breaks out. The point at issue is the vexed question of marriage and divorce. Jewish law was based on the interpretation of Deut 24:1. Divorce is permitted if a man, having married a woman, finds a "shameful thing" (literally, "nakedness of a thing") in her. For the rabbis, depending on their rigidity (school of Shammai) or flexibility and tolerance (school of Hillel), the question centered on what exactly made a wife's conduct improper and so grounds of divorce on the man's part.

The thrust of v. 2 is that Jesus was again put on the spot: or so his enemies imagined. They wanted him to give a ruling on Deut 24:1 and to say what his view of a "shameful thing" was. So they will have material to accuse him of inclining either to the rigorous or lax position. It was a situation where he seemed fated to lose the argument, like "Heads I win, tails you lose!" Notice how he responded:

(a) He declared, in effect, that any kind of divorce is a "shameful thing," since Moses' permission of divorce is only second-best in any case. God's original intention, declared in his will in paradise (Gen 2:24), is that marriage is a partnership for all time, involving a lifelong commitment on both sides and not to be broken. So v. 9 should be rendered: What God has joined together, let not man (i.e., Moses) separate.

(b) The reason for this clear statement is implied. He claims to bring in the age of the Messiah that supersedes the age of Moses by his fulfillment of the law and his returning human society to its "original" relationship to God. The kingdom is thus here, and men and women are called to live under its new order.

(c) In that new age marriage is an equal partnership in which husband and wife stand together before God. This is new teaching, different from contemporary Judaism's preference of a man's rights over a woman's, and it is the main element in Mark's record.

This section has to do with marriage, though 10:9 can be applied in several other ways. What has God joined together? (1) religion and character; (2) faith and reason; (3) the human soul and Jesus. Other linkages are possible: (1) evangelism and social action; (2) spirituality and the secular world; (3) prayer and works.

The Kingdom: Its Appeal (10:13–16)

We recall how this gospel opens with the theme of God's kingdom soon to be set up. The first word Jesus uttered in public promised that God's rule over human lives in an ideal society was near (1:14–15). His parables were all about the kingdom's presence and power (chap. 4). Yet there was deep misunderstanding. This little pericope (10:13–16) illustrates the sort of people that can enter God's realm, since they understand its appeal.

The kingdom belongs to the childlike. Notice it is not childishness that is applauded. What makes children so apt an illustration is not their innocence (a common fallacy!), but their simplicity, gratitude and trustfulness. Above all, little ones do not expect anything from their parents on the score of merit or as a reward for services rendered (they learn that in later life from their grown-ups). They are helpless, and so they are utterly dependent. "Entering the kingdom" like a little child (v. 15) as a text needs to make the exegetical point that, even if the Greek is unclear, the better interpretation is: The kingdom belongs to such as these, the children; and if you do not receive the Father's gift as a child receives gifts from his earthly parent, you will not enter. Then you can itemize the different ways a child "receives" (as suggested above). Most obviously, a child is transparently honest and has no pride, which is the chief barrier to entry into the kingdom of God.

The Kingdom: Its Denial (10:17–27)

Nothing bars the entrance to the kingdom so effectively as self-trust and pride in one's attainments (illustrate from Paul in Phil 3). So we read now as a counterpoint to the above incident how people fail to make it into God's kingdom. The story in these verses is the exact opposite of the one in which the children are blessed; and as is clear, the disciples show up in a poor light once more.

A rich man came running—an unusual feature, since few people ran under the hot Palestinian sun—and wanted a quick answer to a profound question. Here was his first mistake. He is then made to examine his language. He ran up with a flattering remark intended to gain Jesus' approval, "Good Teacher." He is stopped in his tracks by Jesus' refusal to be swayed by this ingratiating praise. Does he really know what "goodness" is? Only one person is perfect goodness and that person is God.

Jesus continues to search his motives. Has he kept the commandments? Yes, comes back the confident response, all except where it really counts, since he doesn't allow Jesus to mention the last item in the Decalogue, "You shall not covet. . . ." He appears on the surface to be a moral and well-adjusted human being, but Jesus says, "You lack one thing." He is still self-sufficient and his trust is in his possessions. Jesus touches him on a tender nerve and calls him to surrender that obstacle that is stopping his commitment to God in full trust. Recall that "Mammon" usually translated "wealth" derives from a Hebrew word for "trust": that's why we cannot serve God and Mammon (Matt 6:24) since trust in one excludes trust in the other. In the case before us, the man had allowed money or possessions to dominate his life: this is the essence of "covetousness," which Paul calls idolatry (Col 3:5) and which Jesus castigated in one of his most forthright stories (Luke 12:13 –21). The answer in this case was for the man to sell all, give it to the needy, and come to join Jesus' disciples.

The challenge evidently proved too costly. The wealthy man loved his possessions, and he went away with clouded face. He trusted in his riches, and his goods became his gods. So sadly the door of the kingdom was barred to him. "The Great Refusal" is a classic sermon title, and we need to explain and illustrate what went wrong. I have suggested some pointers concerning (a) *his priorities* (did he run because this was one engagement in an otherwise busy schedule?) (b) *his flattery*, calling Jesus by a flamboyant title, and (c) *his superficiality*, observing the commandments that pleased him and avoiding the difficult and costly challenge. His action in v. 22 is not unexpected, since already his character was formed and set.

The puzzlement of the disciples (10:28 –31) is understandable once we remember how in the OT riches are a sign of divine favor. In the NT, they are often a barrier to faith, for reasons given in 10:23–27. The rich person finds it hard to enter God's kingdom. To get a camel (the largest animal in Palestine) to pass through the eye of a needle (the smallest aperture the Jews could think of) is to attempt the impossible. Just so, says Jesus, using a current proverb, it is absurd to try to enter the kingdom with a huge bag of wealth strapped to one's person.

"Then, who can be saved?" The disciples ask incredulously. "All things are possible with God" (10:27) is the reply, recalling Gen 18:14. What no human being achieves by merit or strength, God can accomplish in grace.

The Kingdom: Its Costliness (10:32–45)

This section is the third and final prediction of the Passion, and it is the most detailed. Jerusalem is set as the final destination of the journey, for a reason given elsewhere (Luke 13:33). Jesus set his face to the last, fateful journey to the holy city and to his rendezvous with destiny. "The objective is to be Jerusalem; and to go to Jerusalem is to face a violent death" (C. H. Dodd, *The Founder of Christianity*, p. 139).

Mark's account of the fate awaiting him holds nothing back in terms of the horror and indignity to come (10:33–34). We can hardly believe that, with these somber scenes of mockery, disgrace, and physical beating realistically painted, the disciples could be so obtuse and unfeeling as the next episode describes them (10:35–45).

James and John, two of the three privileged disciples, come with a request, "Let us sit one on your right side and one on your left side in your glory." This imagery here, drawn from Jewish ways of arranging seating at a banquet, implies that they wanted to be specially favored at the upcoming celebration. They wanted ringside seats in the extravaganza they expected to witness in Jerusalem. They hoped that Jesus would enter the city in triumph and be hailed as an instant and glorious success. They wanted to be sure of a share in it with him. The other ten disciples were highly indignant, we read—not that they thought differently, but because James and John have jumped to the head of the line and got their applications in first.

Jesus had to clear away misunderstandings. He promised these men the only thing that can be granted: a share in his cup and baptism. They professed a ready acceptance of this arrangement, and we are left to wonder how they came to that position. When they said, "We are able" (v. 39), were they still misguided or did they really comprehend what Jesus was referring to? The answer seems to raise a third possibility, illustrating that we can "hear" an unwelcome message and reinterpret it by decoding it in a way that suits us, and filtering out those elements we find unpleasant. This is what has happened in regard to Jesus' allusion to "his cup" and "his baptism." Both are picture words in the OT for extreme suffering and woe, sometimes involving divine judgment (as in Isa 51:17–18; Ezek 23:31–32; Ps 42:7). Jesus evidently had such pictures in mind as he tried to prepare these men for his destiny at Jerusalem. But James and John "heard" these words in a different way. For them "drinking a cup" meant prosperity and joy (Pss 16:5; 23:5; 116:13) and "baptism" may have suggested a preparatory washing as a way of expecting the coming of the kingdom of God (as the people of the Dead Sea scrolls evidently hoped for). So both metaphors may very well have been decoded as an invitation to get ready for the kingdom which would be celebrated with festivity and joy in Jerusalem.

If this is what they thought, they were grossly mistaken. Their error was the persistent one, made earlier by Peter (8:29, 31–33), of imagining that the time of messianic blessedness could come any other way than by messianic suffering, and that included Jesus and the Twelve. The two disciples are therefore rebuked in v. 40, as Jesus goes on to predict that they will suffer: so it turned out in history. James died a violent death (Acts 12:2) and John was exiled for his faith to a penal settlement on Patmos (Rev 1:9).

The "cup" metaphor is an interesting one in the NT. I have a simple outline on (1) the cup Jesus refused (Mark 15:23); (2) the cup Jesus accepted (Mark 14:36); (3) the cup Jesus instituted (Mark 14:23); (4) the cup Jesus promised (to James and John in this chapter). The theme makes a helpful communion meditation.

The theme of the story returns to discipleship. To be Jesus' authentic follower one must be ready for hardship for the road is hard. It means taking the role of a servant which in turn implies a willingness to be at the disposal of others. Yet the pattern is not one simply described in theoretical or abstract terms. It is fleshed out in the life of Jesus himself. He came not to be served but to serve (v. 45) and to take the part of a slave (v. 44: *doulos* is a stronger term than *diakonos*, mentioned in v. 45). His title to lordship is written in terms of a ministry of service to God and to humankind. To that quality of living he called these men, and he still calls today.

The background of the so-called "ransom saying" in 10:45 is Isa 53, though in current Jewish thought atonement for sin could be secured by at least four methods: repentance, sacrifice, suffering, death. The martyrs and zealots in Israel's history, beginning with Phinehas in Num 25 and climaxing in the Maccabees, were prepared to die for the life of the nation, and a condemned criminal was invited, before his execution, to confess that his death put away his sins. The uniqueness of this "suffering servant" figure in Isa 53 is that he is innocent of crime and is pictured as dying for others. The beneficiaries of his martyr's death include the "many" (Isa 52:14; 53:12), that is, the Gentiles for whom in Judaism there was little if any hope. This is the surprising outreach in Jesus' mission and achievement. He is contemplating a salvation that embraces "the nations" in its scope. As servant of God he will offer himself willingly in sacrificial death, a death which has "unlimited power to atone" for human sins.

His ministry will climax in his death. His whole life has been one of submission to the Father's will and one of self-giving to others—the poor, the needy, the outcast, the sinner. "I serve" (see Luke 22:27) has been his motto all the time. Now he looks forward to the culmination of his ministry and with that a third note is added. To obedience and service is compounded sacrifice as he is prepared to make over his life to deal with sins by consenting to act vicariously on behalf of sinners and to receive the penalty they deserve. The outcome is a deed of saving virtue that is (a) vicarious, "on our behalf"; (b) representative, "in our name"; and (c) sacrificial, as it offers to God an obedience which exhausts the strength of evil and releases a fresh dynamic to break sin's power in human life. These are the three notes that need to be sounded in our attempt to proclaim "Christ Crucified."

But faithfulness to our text requires a fourth dimension. In the context Jesus is not only explaining what his death will

accomplish for his disciples. He is with equal emphasis calling them to share his obedient and sacrificial spirit. Real
"power" is exercised in submission to God's loving design for
our lives and a willingness to yield our rights, just like a slave
(10:43) who has no rights at all. To the above three adjectives
we should add (4) exemplary, as a raison d'être of the cross.
Jesus is teaching and exemplifying a new basis of ethical responsibility. His obedience to death sets a novel pattern
which we are to take as our own. The call is "dying to live" as
we yield our claim to be lord to the service of others and in
obedience to God's will. These few verses help the preacher in
a very difficult task: how is he or she to move from historical
"is"-ness to ethical "ought"-ness, from the factual statement,
"Christ died for me," to the claim that his death impinges on
my life and has existential value and challenge for me today?
The middle term is what we hear as Jesus' call not only to accept his cross and its benefits but also to take up our cross
(8:34) and follow him. Everyone is saved by two crosses:
Christ's and his or her own. Atonement by Christ and new life
in Christ are inextricably linked.

Preaching on 10:45 poses a challenge we ought to accept;
the subject is at the heart of our faith; hence "The Cruciality of
the Cross," as P. T. Forsyth called it. The notes sounded are (1)
authority ("Son of man"); (2) identity ("to serve" by associating with men and women); (3) victory (the servant of God in
Isa 53 emerges from death to new life).

The Kingdom: Its Hope (10:46 –52)

To be his disciple is to be "on the road" that leads to the
cross and beyond. Up to this point the story-line makes dismal
reading. The disciples whom he chose and called remain
dullwitted and hard-hearted (6:51 –52). But there is hope even
if it arises from unlikely places and throws into prominence
unlikely people. The blind beggar shows uncommon perception, as he illustrates one of Mark's favorite themes: faith appears in situations where you least expect it, as we have seen
in 7:24 –30 and 9:14 –27.

Blind Bartimaeus is a nobody on the road of life. His persistent call for help (vv. 47 –48) is an embarrassment to everyone, and they try to hush him. "Don't you know that Jesus has
more important business on hand? He can't be bothered with

wayside beggars and tramps," they might have said. But they
were wrong. Jesus has an interest in just such a person who
knows his need and is made to express the messianic faith in
the Son of David who has come to open blind eyes (Isa 35:5).

"What do you wish me to do for you?" is like a blank
check, reminding us how Jesus wanted always to hear people
specify their request in exact terms. Obviously the man wanted his sight, literally "to see again" or maybe "to lift up his
eyes" in a vision of the spiritual world. He seems the right sort
of candidate, for he makes a statement of faith in Jesus as his
master (v. 51) and Jesus fastened on this "faith" (v. 52). Best of
all, he is ready to follow Jesus "on the road" (of discipleship as
well as of life). Commentators observe Mark's play on words
here. There is the plain sense of a road beside which he has set;
there is a deeper meaning of Jesus' road to Jerusalem and his
destiny. This man is ready for both.

"Insight not Eyesight" might be the sermonic caption of
this miracle tale. Bartimaeus well illustrates (a) Jesus' concern and compassion for one of the most depressed and disad-
vantaged persons in Palestinian society, long before the
arrival of "welfare"; (b) the man's glimmer of faith in recognition and response; (c) his commitment to Jesus' way as a fitting finale. His spiritual vision matches his restored physical
sight. He is like that curious fish in Jacques Cousteau's mari-
time museum that possesses two sets of eyes, one pair for un-
derwater vision and a second pair used when it surfaces. Not
without reason the species is called "Anableps" (the Greek
word for "to see again" or "above," used in our text at vv. 51
and 52).

Bartimaeus' opportunity ("What do you want me to do
for you?") opens up a lot of possibilities: (1) *recognition* in the
crowd, so that he is no longer a cipher; (2) *healing* that will be
his passport into useful life; (3) *purpose,* found in following
Jesus on the road. Here are three universal needs in our day.
Our job as preacher is to make our hearers want what they
need.

The Final Week:
Action and Reaction
(Mark 11:1 — 12:44)

We know that Jesus fell foul of several groups of people. The Pharisees showed their opposition as early in Mark's story as in 3:6. The Sadducees who represented the aristocratic establishment centered on the temple and the sanhedrin also plotted his downfall. There were the Romans whose soldiers carried out the grim sentence of death by crucifixion. The question underlying these factual details is one that congregations often are too timid to ask but one that still lies subsurface. Why did these men oppose Jesus? This section will offer some clues. Such clues are in the shape of action and reaction. Jesus acted in a certain way—by his deeds, his words, his attitudes. The enemies didn't like any of what they saw, heard and understood. So they reacted against him and eventually led him to the cross.

Lord of the Temple (11:1–19)

We usually regard this action as the frontispiece to the Passion, and therefore to be dated on Palm Sunday in the church's liturgical calendar. We see it as providing an object lesson in humility. Jesus condescends to ride into the city on a donkey, not a warrior's horse. But there is symbolism too at work in this narrative. Doubtless the disciples were still thinking in terms of his march on Jerusalem as the grand entrance of the messianic prince, astride a war horse, conquering and to conquer. Instead, he chose the ass as a lowly-beast of burden, and so fulfilled the OT prediction (Zech 9:9 which, however, is not quoted in Mark's account). The crowd too may well have had ideas to make this demonstration a show of popular support for the messianic leader. The starting point from the Mount of Olives—the Hill of Oil as it was called—may have aroused ideas and hopes that this event was to be the entry of the Lord's anointed, based on the current view that Messiah

would stand on this site (Zech 14:4) and proclaim liberty. If
so, the cries of Hosanna ("Save now, we pray") as well as
the leafy branches wafted in mid-air as at the Tabernacles
Feast (Lev 23:40) as a sign of nationalist fervor were probably an embarrassment to Jesus.

It is crystal clear that he had no intention of playing the
part of worldly liberator nor of repeating the Maccabean crusade by resorting to force of arms. His entry was not a stage-
managed bid to be hailed as Messiah nor did he want an
orchestrated "welcome" of this sort. We may therefore question whether "Triumphal Entry" is the correct title for this
story. The disciples and crowd may well have hoped for a triumph; instead they got a down-beat coming to the city on the
back of a lowly donkey.

There are two reasons why we can be pretty sure that this
was the case. First, neither the Jewish authorities nor the Roman military found it needful to take action against what happened. Because there was no official intervention it is clear
that they did not see here any claim, overt or secret, that Jesus
was a king. We know how suspicious the Romans were of
mass rallies of this kind. Secondly, Jesus' main interest on
Palm Sunday was not the city but the temple. He entered the
city to cleanse the sanctuary (11:11, 15). But he did so in a
most unusual way. C. H. Dodd puts it clearly: "The Son of
David was popularly expected to 'cleanse Jerusalem from the
Gentiles.' Jesus wanted it cleansed *for* the Gentiles" (*The
Founder of Christianity*, p. 147). That is, he felt constrained to
cleanse the temple courts of *Jewish* defilements and then to
restore it to its use as a place of worship for the *Gentiles*. In
other words, Jesus turned two popular ideas on their head;
and here are two "points" in any sermon on the Cleansing of
the Temple. Or else we can expand our outline thus: (1) the
temple cleansed; (2) the temple consecrated; and (3) the temple consummated in the "new temple" of Christ's body, the
church (John 2:19–22).

The issue centered on the merchandising and traffic
through the temple forecourt, called the Court of the Gentiles.
It was being used as both an emporium and a shortcut across
the temple mount. Jesus declared that this was a sacred enclo-
sure for prayer, open to anyone and especially non-Jews who

were otherwise excluded. The commercial traffic prevented this; so he put an end to the business which was partly legal (selling sacrificial animals for temple use) and partly corrupt (exchanging coinage into temple currency, at inflated rates). The action of overturning the tables aimed a blow at Sadducean privilege, since the Sadducees were financial officers of the temple and held the purse strings. They kept the exchange business under control and made a fat profit out of it. When he called their place of business "a den of robbers" (11:17) he was using fighting words.

The End of the Nation (11:12–14, 20–26)

His teaching at Bethany was heavy with accents of doom and judgment. The blasting of the fig tree is a difficult incident, since it involved Jesus' dealing destructively with an inanimate object. It seems out of character.

Perhaps the incident is more like an acted parable or dynamic sign, such as the OT prophets performed to illustrate and enforce their message (see, for example, Jer 19 and Ezek 4, 5). The fig tree is a well-known metaphor for the nation of Israel. "Destroying the tree" whose leafless condition showed that it was either dead or dying may be no more than pronouncing a sentence already set; and Jesus was more concerned to warn about the nation's fate. Israel's sorry condition bent on despising God's gracious purpose will lead inevitably to its suffering and destruction, as indeed happened in the fall of Jerusalem in AD 70. The earliest commentator on this gospel, Victor of Antioch (5th century) expressed such a view: Jesus "used the fig tree to set forth the judgment that was about to fall on Jerusalem."

A sermon on "Believing Prayer" is suggested by 11:23–25(26). Notice the conditions to real praying: (1) no half-heartedness; (2) no lack of conviction; (3) no uncharitableness to others. A title like "When Prayer Fails" can meet a pastoral need, rather than "How to Succeed in Praying."

Mark has preserved the teaching, given surely in sadness, not anger or resentment, by Jesus, within a frame of prayer and the need for forgiveness. Above all, there is the call to faith (11:22) which may mean "Cling to God's Faithfulness" in spite of the troubles that loom ahead.

Questions About Authority (11:27–12:12)

These verses entail a scene that raises one of the central issues both for christology and the Christian faith. Where is true authority to be found? It affects our understanding of God, Christ, the Bible, the role of the church and its tradition, and indeed the very substance of religion. In the historical context of the dialogue between the Pharisees and Jesus, the question is sharply framed: "By what authority are you doing these things? Who gave you this authority?" (11:28). What things? Mark doesn't tell us, but he leaves us to infer that it was his actions in cleansing the temple courts. Some interpreters think the episode refers to Jesus' baptizing (as in John 3:22–25), and that would make sense of the allusion to John the Baptist and his washings. Then the Pharisees cannot understand why Jesus permitted his disciples to baptize and they raise the question of John's baptisms.

Jesus picks up the veiled reference to John, and throws it back at them: "When John baptized, did he do it on his own initiative, or did he claim to be acting as God's messenger?" If they say that John was right to baptize because he was a prophet, Jesus will remind them that they didn't accept him as such and in any case John foretold the coming of a greater one (Mark 1:8). If, on the other hand, they attributed no more than human authority to John, they would lose popular support since John's martyrdom was a sacred memory. So they keep a discreet silence when faced with a choice. To men who will not commit themselves to the truth, Jesus will not commit himself. For all such discussions are life-and-death issues, not word games or spinning wheels.

With this background you can develop themes on "Authority: True and False" and "John: A Test Case."

Jesus seems to sidestep the issue in the conflict story of 11:27–33. But he does give an answer later, although it is couched in the form of a parable. He tells the story of the "Owner's Son" partly to take up the challenge thrown down by the question of his authority and partly to justify his messianic mission against his enemies (12:12). While this parable has some features of allegory, it remains a true parable, focusing on a central issue, Who is the son whom the vineyard owner sends "last of all" (v. 6)? Our exposition will

want to identify the various *dramatis personae* of the story:
the owner stands for God; the vineyard is Israel who in her
long history received a succession of prophets and messen-
gers extending from the eighth century BC to John the Baptist; the son represents Jesus who will be given the same
murderous treatment even though he comes as the final
overture of the owner's concern. Notice the historical and
contextual significance of the plan in v. 7. Jewish law main-
tained that, if a property stood without an owner or tenant,
the people who arrived first on the scene can occupy and
claim "squatters' rights." The tenants imagine that if they
reject the owner's delegates one after another and kill the
son, then the property will be theirs since there will be no legal owner with title to the property. What they forget, of
course, is that the owner in a far away country (v. 1) is still
very much alive and well . . . and will act in punitive mea-
sures against these rebellious tenants (v. 9).

The history of Israel is thus encapsulated in this story
with all its tragic depths of refusal and rejection. The drama is
based on Isa 5:1–7 where the end too is a sad verdict of God's
disappointment with the nation. God's character shines
through all his dealings with men and women, in its "kind-
ness and severity—a possible sermon title taken from Rom
11:22. Finally, Jesus' own self-portrait is here in his filial
awareness as an eschatological savior sent "last of all" and in
his confidence of final vindication. The illustration is a vivid
one. The building block that the construction crew refused to
use and cast on one side has become, to their utter amaze-
ment, the keystone of the arch that holds the edifice in place:

> The stone the builders cast aside
> Is now the building's strength and pride.
>
> (Ps 118:22, Moffatt)

After rejection comes reward, as after Good Friday is the
glory of Easter day. This is possible because Jesus is seen to be
none other than God's son, declared to be so by the resurrection of the dead. To tell the story from these three points of
view is to get to the heart of salvation history and to sound the
themes of (a) God's saving purpose; (b) Israel's sad rejection,
which lives on in our refusals and denials today; (c) Jesus' present enthronement and claim as Lord. Or else and more sim-

ply focus on "The Great Reversal" (12:10), and speak of "Jesus
as cornerstone" (1) uniting people to God; (2) cancelling their
alienations from one another; (3) providing a center of worship; using Eph 2:11–22 as illustration.

Appraising the Political Scene (12:13–17)

The tribute money incident shows that the Pharisees were
continuing to be hostile to Jesus and to trap him in debate.
Their subtle, trick question in v. 14 looks easy but it is loaded.
Here was an issue in which any answer seemed to be
incriminating.

We need to comment briefly on the various taxes the Romans imposed as an occupying power: these were the head-
tax, poll-tax, and various sales taxes. All made for a very
heavy burden on the native Jewish population. But the galling
reminder was that God's holy land was under the heel of a pagan power, and resentment was bitter. This gave the nationalist Zealots their keen desire to rebel and free Israel from
foreign domination in the name of Yahweh, the covenant God.
The question of taxation was therefore a much debated issue,
and to open this discussion was to expose a neuralgic nerve.

For Jesus to have said, "Yes, pay the taxes to Caesar"
would be heard as an acceptance of the legitimacy of Roman
rule. This would align him with the Herodians (who were naturally despised) and with the Sadducees who believed in
keeping the status quo. To say, "No, don't pay" would have
the effect of countenancing open revolt and put Jesus on the
side of the Zealots.

Jesus refused to be impaled on the horns of a false dilemma. The question is not one of giving voluntarily to Caesar,
but paying what is due (v. 17). The Jews enjoyed Caesar's gov-
ernment, even if they did not choose to live under it. It gave
them good social order, economic stability (even if the tax bill
ran high) and worldwide peace. Moreover it gave them freedom to practice their religion without harassment, since
throughout the empire Roman law favored Jewish scruples in
diet and sabbath observance. These things had to be paid
for—as we know today and our list can be extended—and the
Pharisees acknowledged this fact by their possession of coins
with Caesar's bust and inscription on them (v. 16).

They admitted to having Caesar's currency, so let them

pay taxes in that coin. Many commentators see a hidden meaning in the next phrase: "Render to God what is his," namely "You carry God's image in your life as his people; Let him be honored by your willing submission." Whether this is a meaningful part of the text is doubtful. What is clear is that Jesus saw no inconsistency between political obligation and religious allegiance (an agreement which Paul also believed, according to Rom 13:1–7). But both Jesus and Paul lived in days before the state turned persecutor and had to be branded as anti-Christ, as in the time of Revelation chapters 13–17 and in more recent examples of totalitarian and fascist regimes.

"Christ and Politics" is an eye-catching title, but it needs to be handled with sensitivity and care, and with a frank admission that the biblical teaching relates to specific historical circumstances which may or may not be the same as those in the world today. Specifically, from the text "Bring me a coin" (12:15), you can tackle the theme of the Christian attitude to money. John Wesley's famous sermon on "The Use of Money" had three points: gain all you can; save all you can; give all you can. Each part needs to be complemented by the other items in the list.

Cynicism and Disbelief (12:18–27)

Still smarting from being labelled keepers of a "den of robbers" (11:17) the Sadducees now mount a counterattack. These leaders of Israel's establishment and defenders of the "old-time religion" accepted only the five books of Moses as binding in matters of faith and practice. In that part of the Bible they professed to find nothing about the afterlife.

So to pour scorn on Jesus' teaching, the Sadducees invented an incredible tale of a woman with seven husbands, each of whom she had married consecutively. "In the resurrection"—which they denied (see Acts 23:7–8)—"whose wife will she be?" They had all married her at one time. Can she be portioned out to them in the next world?

Jesus is a match for them. He doesn't dismiss their story as fantastic (there is a similar tale in the apocryphal book of Tobit, chapter 3). Instead he meets them on their own ground, and he bases his reply on a text from a part of the OT they accepted. In Exod 3, God announced himself to Moses as the God of the patriarchs who lived and died years before him. Yet he spoke in the present tense, "I *am* the God of Abraham," etc. So these patriarchs are not really dead and forgotten. They are alive in God, who keeps them alive in his presence.

The "after-life," as it is popularly called, is a theme of perennial and topical interest. People are interested in all sorts of questions regarding the state of the departed. So here is a chance to make several useful points against the crudely "materialistic" views of the Sadducees and their modern counterparts. Their big mistake was to think only in terms of the future life as an extension or prolongation of existence in this world. Jesus denied that simple equation, and emphasized how in the next life what counts is a new quality of living where earthly ties are different from what we know now. This novelty is "eternal life," real life, richer and deeper than we have ever known because it is life in God whose love cannot be destroyed by death.

The plain teaching of this encounter is (a) there is a life to come, versus Sadducean and materialist unbelief; (b) such life is not this life infinitely prolonged but a new order of existence; and (c) what matters is fellowship with God, untouched by death, that sustains us in his love forever.

Jesus' Question (12:28–37)

After a day of questions comes the "Question of the Day." It was this discussion that really brought matters to a head. Jesus took the initiative and brought the question of his own identity before his hearers. It has been the central issue of Christianity ever since.

Popular expectation centered in a coming "Son of David" or Messiah, a hope going back to 2 Sam 7:11–16 and developed by the prophets of Israel and especially at Qumran and among the Pharisees who prayed the sentence, "Look, O Lord, and raise up for them their king, the Son of David." In all of this hope the Messiah is pictured as a political, earthly and nationalist leader.

The point of the dialogue in this section is: how can David's son, the Messiah, be both a descendent of David (and so inferior to him) and one to whom David looked up and called Lord (as in Ps 110:1)? Jesus posed this question to the embarrassment of his critics. They have no answer, since they will persist in their understanding of the deliverer as a politi-

cal or earthly figure. Jesus, in effect, denied this. True, he has
come as a loyal son of Israel, born of David's family (as in the
birth stories), but he is no worldly liberator as the Zealots
wanted, nor a supporter of the status quo as the Sadducees
hoped for, nor a religious teacher whose "orthodoxy" stayed
within the limits of the Pharisees' tradition. He is much more
than an earthly Messiah. He is "the Man who fits no formula,"
to use E. Schweizer's nice phrase. That's because he is David's
Lord and God's own son.

A sermon on christology from the text, "What do you
think of Christ?" is really ready-made from this background.
All you need to do is to sketch the current options: Jesus as political "liberator," as ecclesiastical dignitary, as religious con-
formist, and show how these options still apply as he is
claimed as patron in our world and by today's church. But he
refuses to be categorized in any of these ways. His true title is
"Lord" and that means he is both critic and criterion of all political, social and religious systems. "Lord" is essentially an
appellation of authority and ownership, and asserts his right-
ful—because God-given—power to rule. The Lordship of
Christ is therefore (a) declared on the cross; (b) decided by the
resurrection (quoting Rom 1:3–4; Phil 2:9–11; 2 Tim 2:8) and
(c) demanded of the church and the Christian (Rom 14:9) in
life and death. He seeks not our admiration but our adoration;
not our patronage, but our obedience. Sometimes that obedience can be costly, as seen in the German Confessing church in
the 1930's and in Baptist groups in Russia in our day.

"You are not far from the Kingdom of God" (12:34) looks
to be a promising verse, commending the man. But it is quali-
fied by a reminder that "not far" is not "inside"; though there
is encouragement to think the man was on the right track.
Here are several sermon pointers.

A Look Ahead
(Mark 13:1–37)

All commentators agree that Mark 13 is the most difficult part of the gospel to understand, as most preachers will confess to a puzzlement often leading to a near-paralysis when their minds try to get to grips with what the text can mean to a modern audience.

One suggestion that may help is the idea of a vision. Our eyesight, in default of clear 20-20 vision, needs the assistance of lenses to correct and improve that vision. Bifocal lenses enable us to adjust the focal length of our eyesight to see near and then distant objects. Now come trifocal lenses for even better adjustment, covering near, middle and far distances. That's exactly what we need to wear (figuratively speaking), when we come to look at Mark 13.

There are three "ranges" of vision.

(a) Much of what Jesus alluded to in this recorded teaching concerned the immediate situation and experience of the apostolic church (13:5–13).

(b) A more distant scene is included in the predictions of the fall of Jerusalem, preceded by the Jewish war of AD 66–70 (13:14–23).

(c) There is a more distant focus that extends to the "end of the age" (13:24–27), described in heavy apocalyptic language.

Then we need to keep switching from one lens to another in vv. 28–31, with the last section (vv. 32–37) covering both the time in the unknown future (v. 32) and the immediate situation that requires the disciples' continual alertness (vv. 33–37).

As in the parables chapter of Mark 4 and the controversy stories (in chapters 1–3, 11, 12), the evangelist may have put together into a convenient compendium an assortment of Jesus' prophetic sayings addressed to different themes and audiences. This suggestion makes it important for us to use the trifocal lenses today as we try to decide which time-frame best suits the particular verses of this enigmatic chapter.

Its enigma is not helped by the use of OT and Jewish apocalyptic terms, in particular drawn from the book of Daniel. This is a descriptive form of writing, combining symbolism and other-worldly features, by which the end of the age is depicted, but with reference to this world. We need this warning against excessive literalism and the misuse of apocalyptic as a kind of secret code by which we feed the fires of idle curiosity and needless speculation. The purpose of apocalyptic was serious and practical: it was to encourage the faithful to endure in the hope that God's purposes would surely prevail and his rule be vindicated on earth. But true hopes need to be separated from false ideas and bogus promises. So the apocalyptic writings, both Jewish and Christian, are studded with warnings to put God's people on their mettle: "Take heed that no one leads you astray."

The First Vision (13:5–13)

Jesus' forecast that the temple would be torn down in ruins (13:1–2) fell as bad news on the ears of faithful Jews. Naturally they wanted to know more, and in particular when will these catastrophes occur? Notice how the language of the disciples' request for information is taken directly from Dan 12:7. That is the hermeneutical key to the entire discourse, set on the Mount of Olives where divine revelation was supposed to take place in the last days, according to Zech 14.

Jesus' response is couched in terms of warning. Let the disciples not jump to hasty conclusions, he says, forewarning them that soon after his departure, they would be in danger of being led astray. Bogus prophets will appear, proclaiming the end of the world and laying claim to exalted titles ("I am" is God's own name, according to Exod 3:14). There is historical evidence in a sad succesion of megalomaniac prophets from Bar Kokba in AD 135 to Jim Jones of Jonestown, Guyana in our time. Tragic results always follow.

Natural disasters equally are part of our human story, and disasters bring suffering (famine, disease, death) in their wake. These events happen all the time, and they are no indication that "the end" is near. The next kind of suffering (v. 9) is more bitter, when it involves trial and persecution. The good news must be offered to all peoples prior to "the end." So it means that when phony prophets proclaim

that the end of the age is around the corner, they are not to
be trusted.

The proclamation of the message will sort our families
and friends. Christians will have to accept misunderstanding,
loss and even hatred on the part of their kinsfolk. It is because
of their first loyalty to Jesus Christ (v. 13). So the Twelve are
called to be courageous when they face a hostile world. As
they go out as missionaries, they must expect hardship and
physical suffering. But they have a secret "armory" in their
defense and hidden resources on which they can draw (v. 11).
The promise of God's help is the Holy Spirit who will give the
best equipment: readiness to endure the trial and win through
to the end.

Three ways the Spirit assists believers in this context are
suggested: (a) insight and perception, to discern who are the
true and who are the counterfeit prophets in our day; (b) courage to take a stand for Christ and his cause; and (c) perseverance, to maintain our trust until the end.

The Second Vision (13:14–23)

The angle of Jesus' vision changes, and the text looks
ahead to the events leading up to AD 70. "The desolating (or
appalling) sacrilege" (v. 14) is a famous phrase that goes back
to Dan 9: 27; 11:31; 12:11 and 1 Maccabees, where it speaks of
an act of desecration that rendered the Jerusalem temple defiled. Specifically it was Antiochus' trespass and sacrifice of a
pig on Yahweh's altar. It left the Jews horror-struck. We read
on that after the Maccabean victory this defilement was removed and the temple sanitized (1 Macc 4:36–54).

Various attempts have been made to relate the reference
in the gospels to some historical occasion. There are three
main options. One is that the phrase witnesses to the attempt
of the mad emperor Caligula to set up his statute in the temple
in AD 40. Another sees the allusion as referring to the stress of
Jerusalem under Roman siege in AD 66–70. The clown Phanni
was mockingly crowned (according to Josephus) and sacrile-
giously dressed up as high priest and installed in the sacred
office. The third possibility is the bringing in of the Roman
standards to the temple precincts at the victorious conclusion
of the war. Whatever the precise detail, it relates to the horror
Jewish pietists (or Jewish Christians among them) felt by the

Roman attack on the central and most holy place of their
religion.

The thrust of Jesus' warning is to make his people ready
to expect further troubles at the outbreak of the Roman war.
For Jewish Christians there was one ray of hope. They received a message by a prophet (sometimes thought to be
based on Mark 13:14) that they should quit Jerusalem and escape to Pella, a town in Transjordan.

But no such way of escape was evidently taken by the
Jews living in the holy city. They were doomed once the Roman legions encircled Jerusalem, and in spite of the courageous last stand at Masada in the desert they perished in great
numbers. Those who survived lived to recall the vain hopes of
leaders and prophets whose words they feebly trusted. But
Jesus was warning them in advance (v. 23).

The Third Vision (13:24–27)

Our understanding of this central section will have to be
governed by our answer to a single question: Is Jesus still continuing his warnings regarding Jerusalem's fall or does his vision (or that of some prophetic spirit speaking on his
authority) shift to engage the drama of the end of history, its
denouement? In the second case, the rationale for placing the
section here ties in with Jesus' warnings of the onset of false
Christs and deceiving signs (v. 22) and "in those days" is the
editorial link-phrase. A pointer in the direction of a non-literal
interpretation is the attested manner in which symbols such
as the sun and moon failing, and the stars falling from their
sockets, as well as "the clouds" (v. 26) which attend a divine
epiphany are all used in the OT. These cosmic phenomena can
have figurative meanings (as in Isa 13:10; 24:21–23; 34:4). But
some historical event is clearly in mind when the text speaks
of the "coming of the Son of man" and we are driven to a
choice that what is in view is either the final parousia of Christ
in his glory or his enthronement following the ascension. The
writer in Dan 7:13 seems to have the latter scenario in his
mind, and the exaltation of the human figure to the throne of
God is precisely what the symbolisms of 13:26 relate to (Acts
1:9–11). This interpretation is clinched by the same "Son of
man" imagery in Mark 14:62 and it gives tolerable sense to
that "exegetical crux" in 13:30. "This generation" can be tak-

en in its natural sense to mean that the hearers of Jesus' words will live on to his ascension and enthronement which, in turn, mark the beginning of that segment of history which will run on to include "the last days." "All these things" that are destined to happen refer primarily to the events of AD 33 and AD 66–70, and they are a prism through which Jesus the prophet sees unfolding the drama of the wind-up of history.

Preaching the eschatological message of Jesus is a risky business, and we must resist the temptation to over-interpret the text. Exegetical overkill is a preacher's hazard in this area. What can be said would include: (a) Christ is the Lord of history, fulfilling himself throughout its long haul until the climax. (b) History, as the believer sees it, is a series of highs and lows, or marked by an ebb and flow rhythm (to use K. Scott Latourette's imagery) of success and failure, advance and reverse, prosperity and persecution. The "end time" simply intensifies these polarities, and the dramatic finale is set at a time no one knows (v. 32). Elements of surprise and unexpectedness are in the exquisite "Parable of the Porter" (13:33–37) as they are in the entire NT witness. Finally (c) Christian watchfulness and conscientious service are the order of the day (v. 37), whether the master comes soon or late. And an essential ingredient of this attitude is clear-sighted, level-headed common sense.

The most helpful text in this chapter is "he who endures to the end will be saved" (13:13). "Endurance"—a dogged determination not to quit—is a key word in the NT. It is a quality (1) demanding *courage;* (2) calling us to *obedience;* (3) yet supplying us with *a model,* Jesus the one who held out to the end (Heb 12:1, 2: note that "perseverance" and "endured" in RSV are from the same Greek term). So "His Persistence and Ours" are matched, and this can be related to Mark 13.

The Upper Room, the Garden, and the Trial Scene
(Mark 14:1–72)

R. H. Lightfoot (*History and Interpretation in the Gospels* [London: Hodder and Stoughton, 1934] p. 141) makes a summarizing statement that may introduce the so-called Passion narrative. "The passion is the supreme act of the Messiah, and conversely the Messiahship of Jesus is the explanation of the passion." The sentence just quoted holds together a cluster of ideas we can profitably explore in any proclamation of Jesus' last days. One serviceable way to explain Mark's intention as an evangelist is to contrast Palm Sunday with the meals at Bethany (14:1–9) and the upper room (14:12–25).

Jesus entered Jerusalem to the shouts of Hosanna (11:9). Those cries were associated with the Feast of Tabernacles which celebrated Israel's patriotic destiny. Doubtless the people who lined the route were full of expectation that their deliverance from political oppression was at hand. If so, they were in for a letdown. Rather, Jesus saw his destiny in connection with the Passover, and in that light he re-interpreted the meaning of messiahship. So the gospel writer adds a time-notice as the frontispiece of his Passion story (14:1–2). We could describe Jesus' intention simply as the joining together of Messiah and Passover. These are the two ideas or leading themes of our chapter. And there are three places where the two ideas run together.

A Woman Proclaims His True Identity (14:3–9)

The anointing at Bethany is rich in acted symbolism and dramatic theology. The pointers are directed to the momentous proposition that Jesus went to his death as God's chosen agent, the Messiah of Israel. We can focus on the woman, to start with. (a) *Her action* is well-described and in some detail. She came to the meal table and broke the flask of precious perfume over his head. This act looks clearly like an anointing of the Israelite (messianic) king as in 2 Kings 9:1–13 (see 1 Sam

10:1). The woman had glimpsed who Jesus was, namely the true King of Israel and had supplied the consecrating oil to proclaim his "messiahship" ("Messiah" means the "anointed" by God).

The bystanders see nothing of this. They are looking only at a disgraceful waste of a priceless commodity, and the woman is under attack for a senseless, wasteful action. Jesus rallies to her defense (v. 6), calling her sacrifice a "lovely deed," and for one special reason. (b) *Her perception* was clear-sighted; this is why she had poured the aromatic oil over his head, thereby confessing faith in him as God's anointed one. But her faith was directed to a suffering Messiah, for she had prepared his body for burial after death (v. 8) and had offered a "work of love" at some cost to herself, not simply a "gift of love" which could be no more than an emotional outburst on the spur of the moment. The Jewish rabbis made a clear distinction between these two types of action, ranking the duty of love higher than a gift which expressed affection and sympathy. Mark intends us to see much more than a spontaneous and effusive display of affection; the woman is the first individual to perceive the person of Jesus as crucified Messiah.

(c) *Her service* played a historic part in the ongoing purposes of God, since what she did brought Jesus one step further to an appointment with his saving destiny. That's why he gave the woman a high place in history and remarked that her deed would be memorialized forever (v. 9)—a prophecy that on face-value seems so unlikely, but in fact is self-fulfilled every time we read this story, whether in private or liturgically.

These three motifs can well be our sermon division for an exposition of "A Woman to Remember." Judas' dastardly deed, the antithesis of sacrifice, can be used as counterpoint (14:10–11).

The Disciples Celebrate the Passover (14:12–25)

There are some historical difficulties with precisely identifying Jesus' last meal with the regular Passover. (14:12 seems to be at odds with the notice in 14:2 which says that the Jewish leaders wanted to arrest Jesus *before* the Passover season.) Whatever the specific day, it does seem clear that in the upper room the disciples were ready to celebrate the family Passover, perhaps as an antedated service, prior to the regular feast. The Jewish Passover still has a two-way look. Faithful Jews take a long glance back into their past history and recall how God brought their fathers out of Egypt (Exod 12; Deut 16). The God of the OT is always the "out-of-Egypt-bringing God," as German scholars can express it. Then, pious Jews peer expectantly into the future and sigh for their promised redemption from bondage. The one item that binds together past and future is their special relationship to God, known as the share they have in his covenant. So Passover has three "moments" in the ritualized drama: thanksgiving, covenant, hope.

Jesus performed actions with the Passover cups and dishes, but gave fresh meaning by the novelty of his words. These "interpreting words" give a clue to what this Passover was all about.

(a) The covenant (in v. 24) centers in his person, symbolized in the bread he handed to the disciples with the words, "This is my body" (v. 22). We should see here an acted parable of Jesus' death by which he was extending to these men a share in his self-offering on the cross. As they eat the bread, they gain a share in him and his death, for "the body" is Jesus himself. We can recognize the semitic usage of "the body = self" in the English word "everybody" = every one.

(b) The covenant is sealed in blood, as was the Mosaic compact at Sinai (Exod 24). But this is no animal blood used to ratify the agreement as when Moses took the sacrificial blood and sprinkled it on the book and the people. Jesus has woven together in a single statement the images of Exod 24:8 and Isa 53:12 as he talks of "my blood of the covenant, which is poured out on behalf of many." The "many" are the Gentiles, destined to share in the blessings of Messiah's death. The members of Mark's church would instantly recognize this fact in their reciting these words at their eucharistic services.

(c) The covenant brings the disciples into a new relationship with Jesus beyond death (v. 25). He says that he will greet them again in the new age of his kingdom soon to be established.

So the "last supper" has distinct overtones that are carried forward to the church's "Lord's supper" celebration. It was a sacrifice in which believers have a share; it renewed the covenant, setting it on a new basis as Messiah's death re-

deemed the world from the power of sin; and it promised a reunion with Jesus in a joyous fellowship beyond the cross.
These are the pledges Jesus gave at the last meal; and for the
church "the reality behind the rite" is one of celebration, in
company with the living Lord and his people, of all he has ac-
complished by his messianic death and victory.

The men to whom Jesus first gave these pledges were no
better and no worse than his modern disciples. Peter is a case
in point. His protestations of loyalty (v. 29) are matched by
Jesus' realistic statements that Peter is no different from other
men. He too will fail and fall away before the drama is over, a
time signalled by the "crowing of the cock" (v. 30). Normally
this allusion is taken to be the rooster's early morning call,
but it may conceivably refer to the Roman bugle call from
midnight to 3 a.m. which had the name "cock-crow" (Latin
gallicinium). The Passion story is punctuated by various
sounds and noises, mostly human but occasionally not, like
the cock crow, as usually understood.

The sad denials of Peter (14:66–72) are intensified by
their repetition, involving him in a standoff with a female servant and a bystander who recognized that he is a Galilean (by
his accent; Matt 26:73). His courage, seen by his presence in
the courtyard, at length failed him when the interrogation became pointed. "The Disciple and the Bird" joins Peter's behavior, fall, and recovery to the cock crowing. There are three
points of contact: (1) The bird's call reminded him of his
prideful *self-assurance*, as we say, "cock-sure" (14:29); (2) The
cock's shrill call should have awakened *vigilance*. Atop a stee-
ple the weather-cock gives a clue to the weather prospects; (3)
the rooster's early morning crow is a sign of *hope*, heralding
the new day. For Peter's three denials there will be a threefold
commission (John 21:15–17).

Jesus Prays in the Garden (14:32–42)

A once-popular song carried the line, "One is nearer God's
heart in a garden, Than anywhere else on earth." That's a nice
sentiment, yet probably untrue—unless it is the particular
garden of Gethsemane. We are there on holy ground, with a
scene that touches the depths of human stress, sacrifice and
obedience. The centerpiece is the prayer (v. 36) that the cup
should be removed, followed by the Lord's submission to the

Father's holy will. I suggest that the key, however, lies in the prefacing words, "All things are possible to you" (v. 36a).

The words point to Jesus' conviction that God's kingdom will come in God's own way. That chosen path will certainly include physical suffering and death; it will entail the grim prospect of Jesus' becoming denied the Father's face as he accepts the role of savior and vicarious sufferer. Out of that experience he will utter a prayer of desolation, based on Ps 22:1 (Mark 15:34). So "the cup" is usually associated with (a) human suffering and (b) divine judgment and wrath. There is ample precedent in the OT for such meanings to be given to the metaphor. I suggest, however, that there is a third possibility. (c) The cup could conceivably be a vivid expression of his experience of satanic temptation. Gethsemane, in this view, is indeed the place of conflict as Jesus for the final time wrestled with the demonic insinuation that he could tread God's path and still avoid the cross.

Throughout his ministry he had been tempted to fulfill his mission in a way that would have gained him an immediate and popular response. You can illustrate this in three ways. First, he could have offered his critics an accrediting sign from heaven (8:11–13). Second, he might have capitalized on his miracle-working power and commanded a following among the people who would have greeted him as a new king who came to usher in an age of plenty and prosperity, with freedom from Roman rule an added bonus (6:30–44). Third, he would have received the plaudits of his own disciples if he had promised them thrones (10:37) and good seats in the spectacle of an imminent kingdom. But he consistently refused these false trails.

Instead, he set his face to serve God's kingdom in God's way; and in a mystery he knew that this would entail his obedience unto death. Now, within the shadow of the cross, he faced the ultimate trial. The pressure to turn back is at its strongest as the hour of final obedience comes; and it is the time of satanic testing which is represented by the cup. So he prayed for its removal as for the passing of the hour of trial (v. 35). The disciples too are involved (v. 38), for in a real sense they would choose, if they could, an easy road for him and themselves. He called them to "keep watch and pray, lest [they] come to the test."

Jesus won through to a final oblation of his will to God; and in an ultimate submission he yielded his life to God as his obedient and trustful son and servant. The victory of the cross is already achieved in the garden. Put epigrammatically, the sermon title of this text has to be "The soul of his suffering was the suffering of his soul."

The Sanhedrin Condemns Jesus (14:53–56)

This section serves one purpose, namely to show how Jesus was condemned by the Jewish court and finally rejected as Israel's Messiah. The proceedings are more like an arraignment than an official trial. The object seems to have been to fasten some accusation of indictable offense on Jesus, which will make it inevitable that he should be transferred to Pilate's court.

We can show the evidence for this way of regarding the text from one or two examples. A trial at night was contrary to strict legal procedures. If the Jewish authorities had in fact tried Jesus and found him guilty (as they did, according to v. 64), why did they not proceed immediately to carry out the sentence of death? This would have been by stoning, the prescribed penalty for blasphemy (Lev 24:10–23). The answer has to be that this scene was not a formal capital trial; and in any case it seems likely that the sanhedrin did not have, at that time, the power to pass the death sentence and carry it out (as John 18:31–32 observes).

What was the charge levelled at Jesus? Mark's Gospel describes it in terms of blasphemy (14:64). The claim to be the Messiah would not, technically speaking, lead to a charge of blasphemy. So it was more likely Jesus' insistence that he would overthrow the temple and would build another temple, altogether divine ("made without hands"). Some scholars (such as Vincent Taylor) propose that the incriminating claim he made was to be a sharer of the divine throne, the Son of man in Dan 7 (so 14:62). Yet again it has been argued that Jesus' silence was his offense because it put him in contempt of court and made him a rebel against the highest Jewish authority. On any of these charges, however unjustifiably made, Jesus could have been "condemned to death," and his case remitted to Pilate, the Roman prefect who alone had the power to authorize an execution in Israel at that time.

"The trial of Jesus," however, is a much wider issue than the legality and circumstance of his appearing before the sanhedrin. A good series of sermons can be worked out on the general theme of the suffering Christ, taking its cue from this chapter. What exactly constituted the "suffering of his soul"? We can itemize (and you can elaborate) the following: (a) He bore the cowardice of Peter with composure, when lesser men would have collapsed under the weight of a broken friendship and a cruel desertion. (b) In his mind there would be mingled sorrow and pain over Judas who betrayed him (14:43–49). The mystery of Judas remains as a solemn warning to all, yet we cannot escape the grim irony of the garden treachery. Not with a shout, a blow, or a stab *(et tu, Brute)*—but with a kiss, the token of love and endearment, the Son of man is betrayed (James S. Stewart). And Judas goes off to collect the fee for services rendered. (c) The publicity and shame of the trial before the Jewish council must have struck deep into the loyal heart of Jesus. Most people feel a sense of remorse and shame when caught on the wrong side of the law. A traffic cop's siren warning us to "pull over" after a speeding offense makes many of us initially blush! But Jesus is put "on trial" faced by trumped-up charges and listens to his words as they are wrenched from context and distorted as "evidence" against him. He suffered the indignity of a question (v. 61) designed simply to incriminate him. (d) But his greatest trial was the agony in the garden. Emphasize that it was a "conflict" (Greek *agon*, "conflict" which Luke 22:44 mentions), not a charade. It was a real struggle, not a piece of play-acting. He was victorious, but only because he was determined to accomplish the Father's purpose, see it through to the end, and maintain a firm constancy of will. A sermon on "Temptation" should include these essential points, drawing on the paradigm of Jesus' struggle in Gethsemane.

"The Tempted Christ" is also an appropriate text for a sermon on Gethsemane. Somehow the theme has to be related to our experience: (1) temptation is an experience common to all (1 Cor 10:13); Jesus was truly man; (2) temptation lies chiefly in preferring "my will" to God's; Jesus resisted at that point; (3) temptation is overcome by constancy of the human will; Jesus entered on life with a resolve, "I come to do your will, O God" (Heb 10:7–9).

The Day of the Cross
(Mark 15:1–47)

In 1909 William M. Clow, a notable Scottish preacher, published a volume of sermons under the title *The Day of the Cross* (London: Hodder and Stoughton). The organizing theme of these pulpit utterances was to see the personalities of the Passion as providing a window of access to the mind of the Lord himself. Modern study of the gospels has strikingly endorsed this purpose. The men and women who appear on the stage, and even those who have "speaking parts" to play do so, not for their own sake but in order to help the reader see more of what the cross meant to Jesus himself. The church that reads the story derives strength and encouragement from this record of the Lord's suffering under trial as it identifies, in its experience of persecution, with him. For a suggestive treatment of Mark in particular, from such a perspective, see Hans-Ruedi Weber's *The Cross* (Grand Rapids: Eerdmans, 1979) pp. 38–40, 103–10.

A quick reading of the Good Friday drama might suggest a different conclusion. We might suppose that it is other people who are wielding the power and tugging at the puppets' strings. Jesus seems to be caught in the vortex of a political struggle of Jews versus Romans, and to be the victim of circumstances that swirl around him. But this is not so. He is still Lord, even if he allows his enemies to have their way with him. In a strange phenomenon in this gospel account the Markan Jesus speaks only three times and that briefly after his arrest in the garden (14:62; 15:2, 34). Repeatedly when provoked or invited to speak, he maintains a passive silence, as we see from 15:5 and especially 15:29–32 where for the final time his enemies taunt him and call on him, mockingly, to give a sign. But he is still uncooperative with the demand for a validating sign, as before (8:11–13).

Mark's readers would find immense comfort and strength at this point. They were experiencing suffering and persecution when for the first time the emperor Nero began to punish them with death as an act of imperial policy. No doubt, they

too were asking, "My God, why have you forsaken us?" like
the martyrs who cry out in Rev 6:9–11. The answer comes
back: Be patient and courageous, and God will bring you
through suffering to glory, just as he did the Lord himself. Also, they would recall the example of Jesus himself who did not
answer back when he was incriminated but endured to the
end. Notice how 1 Peter—a document which tradition associates with Mark in time and circumstance—encourages Christians in persecution with precisely this appeal to the picture
of the suffering Jesus (1 Pet 2:20–23; 3:15–17).

Sermons on the passion of Jesus come in all styles and
configurations. There are topical addresses which highlight
the personality and emotional reaction of the *dramatis personae*, as there are doctrinal expositions that explore the theological weight of Jesus' desolation and despair (Mark 15:34).
Mark's Gospel, it seems to me, stresses the hortatory aspects
of Jesus' death much more prominently, and it is this feature,
called in modern study the *parenetic* significance of the narrative, that should figure in our treatment. We can take several
illustrations of this from chapter 15.

Jesus and Pilate (15:1–20)

As we saw, the charge levelled at Jesus before the Jewish
council was blasphemy. Now as the case is taken to the Roman prefect, it is high treason against the state. Jesus, it was
alleged, claimed to be "king of the Jews"; and that title was
one that Pilate was bound to take notice of, given the sensitivi-
ties of the Jewish authorities and the liability of rebellion
against Rome to break out at the least pretext.

Yet Pilate was caught in a delicate situation. His own position was weak, since he had lost a patron in Rome with the
downfall of Sejanus in recent days. Sejanus had influenced
the emperor Tiberius in an anti-Semitic direction; but now
with Sejanus' influence gone, the emperor was more favora-
bly disposed to the Jews. The last thing Pilate wanted in the
Judean province was trouble at the Passover of AD 33. It was
bad news indeed when the Jewish leaders came, in the early
morning, with a charge he could not safely ignore.

He tried to get himself off the hook by offering to release
Jesus and transfer the blame to Barabbas who was awaiting
execution as an insurgent rebel in a Roman death-row (15:6–

15). This appeal to a "paschal amnesty," in spite of its historical difficulty, stands in Mark's narrative as a desperate expe-
dient to solve Pilate's problem. We glimpse here his strange,
vacillating behavior that historians have found to be quite un-
becoming and bizarre in a stern Roman official.

When all else failed, Pilate had no choice but to pass
sentence. No choice that is, provided he was prepared to
put prestige, rank and security before the dictates of conscience, duty and truth. But that was the price he was willing to pay. He goes down in history—as memorialized in
the Apostles' Creed ("suffered under Pontius Pilate")—as
that Roman governor whose weak will and selfish ambi-
tion allowed him to compromise his conscience in order to
retain his earthly status. Here is a paradox a sermon on Pilate can develop. Statesmen and leaders who can be cor-
rupted are the worst possible kind.

There is a further paradox to be seen in the soldiers'
mockery, based evidently on a mock "carnival of the king."
Prisoners were dressed in royal robes and greeted as though
they were Caesar (*Ave Caesar* becomes "Hail, king of the
Jews," in v. 18). The "crown of thorns" is a caricature of the
radiate laurel crown worn by the emperor as a sign of his divine kingship. The soldiers pressed it on Jesus' head as a cruel
parody and crude joke. But whatever the intent of the crown
of thorns, Christians have always seen it as a token of the
crown Jesus rightly wears:

> The head that once was crowned with thorns
> Is crowned with glory now.

This can be worked in a sermon on "Wearing the Crown," in
its disgrace and glory. And it leads on to the Pauline teaching
of "If we suffer with him, we shall be glorified with him"
(Rom 8:17).

Jesus and Simon (15:21–26)

Another man in the scenario is Simon of Cyrene, a place
in North Africa (see Acts 2:10). He apparently lived in Jerusalem or else its environs. He had come to the city for the feast.
But the interest of Mark's readers would be drawn directly to
the names of his sons, Alexander and Rufus. The latter name
appears in Paul's letter to the Romans (16:13) where greetings

are sent to a certain Rufus. Commentators consider it very possible that this man is the same as the one mentioned by Mark. He was a member of the church in Rome.

It becomes a useful lead-in to a character-study to dramatize how Rufus' father had the honor of carrying the crosspiece called a *patibulum* that all condemned criminals were compelled to bear to the place of execution. And that honor, though forced on Simon ("they commandeered him," v. 21—a military word), was gladly received, we may believe, even if he was a "foreigner." Mark's overall purpose in highlighting the place of unusual persons in the gospel drama is seen here. But more impressively, Simon makes good the sombre prophecy of Jesus: "If any man would come after me, let him deny himself *and take up his cross* and follow me" (8:34). Many in Mark's own church were doing what that word of discipleship implied. They were dying for their faith at the time of Nero's persecution against the church in Rome. They would recall Simon, the father, as a man they knew well, and take courage. So Simon's (a) privilege, (b) courage and (c) example shine out clearly in this pericope as Jesus moves on his way to Calvary and his appointment with destiny as "righteous sufferer" (Ps 22) and savior (v. 31).

The mystery of his dying cry in v. 34 has provoked much wonder and puzzlement. "God, forsaken by God," asked Luther, "How can it be?" "It was as though God turned atheist," commented Dorothy L. Sayers. Our study of the "cry of desolation" should include the following pieces of data: (a) It is a recitation of the opening of Ps 22 which describes the righteous sufferer in Israel who, in the end, wins through to victory. (b) If it is true that Jesus saw his messianic vocation in terms of second Isaiah's suffering servant, then part of that destiny was that his soul is made "an offering for sin," as the "ransom for many" (10:45). (c) The value of this grim scene includes the way it would speak to the church's needs in time of persecution when many Christians were doubting their faith. To be assured that the Lord cried out in his God-forsakenness, but was brought through to final vindication would lift the spirits of Christians and give them grounds for faith even when God seemed far away and there was no immediate deliverance. The experience of the martyrs in every age, of Jews in

Auschwitz and Dachau and of Christians in Gulag Archipel-
ago, brings this thought up-to-date.

Jesus and the Centurion (15:38–39)

The man was evidently the officer who was in charge of
the execution squad. Throughout the grim ordeal of crucifixion (a method of capital punishment the Romans regarded
with distaste and horror, as Cicero tells us), he was impressed
by all that had taken place before his eyes and ears. He
couldn't understand (Mark tells the reader) the darkness (v.
33), the demeanor of the crucified and his expiring cry (v. 39),
and perhaps the message of the inscription fixed over his
head, giving the accused man's crimes (v. 26). He was in an
impressionable mood, and his confession was, "Truly this
man was God's son" (v. 39).

Any sermon on "The Centurion at the Cross" gives us opportunity to observe several things. First, Mark has skillfully
placed a single verse (39) in close connection with what pre-
cedes, which in turn interrupts the flow of the story. The sequence is artistic. We hear Jesus' cry. Then our attention is
diverted to the temple area and to the most holy place where
the separating curtain is torn by an unseen hand, as if to sym-
bolize a breaking down of the barrier that kept men and wom-
en from God's presence (the curtain referred to in Heb 10:19–
22). Finally, we revert to the scene on the hill, and we learn
that it is a pagan soldier who first benefits from this new access to God. He enters the holy place and, with the Christian
confession on his lips—the attestation of faith in Jesus as son
of God that runs through Mark's Gospel from start (1:1) to finish—he becomes the first convert to the faith. Moreover, he is
the initial sign of the great Gentile ingathering to the church
from the Roman world. Familiar with the idea that the Roman emperor is a son of the gods (*divi filius*), this man now ut-
ters the confession that brought Christians into direct
collision with the worship of the emperor (the evidence is in 1
John, the Revelation, and the Martyrdom of Polycarp—all
good illustrative materials). There is no king but Jesus. He
alone is God's son. Mark's church would need and profit from
this encouragement at a time of missionary expansion to the
Greco-Roman world and state persecution. The words on the
centurion's lips are a promise and pledge of a harvest yet to be
reaped and a reminder that we should not despair of God's

cause nor doubt the crucified's ultimate victory. There is thus (a) an *apologetic* interest in this story, showing that a Roman soldier can find no crime in Jesus; and (b) a *soteriological* theme, illustrating how through the torn curtain entrance into God's presence is now available to all, irrespective of race or background. The "open sesame" formula is the confession of Jesus as divine son. (c) There is equally a *missiological* motif, promising a worldwide church that reaches out to embrace the entire Gentile world. Of that universal society the centurion is a charter member.

Jesus and Joseph (15:42 –47)

Yet one more "personality of the Passion" contributes his meaning to Jesus' death. Joseph of Arimathea boldly came to Pilate to gain permission to bury Jesus' body (vv. 23, 24). Pilate expressed surprise that Jesus had died so quickly. Victims often lingered on the cross for several days.

We remember the indignity in the ancient world attaching to an unburied corpse. The issue is the theme of Sophocles' play *Antigone.* So Joseph's action had a deep meaning. The fact that Pilate agreed says two things: (a) It shows that he thought Jesus was no common criminal, for such men were consigned to a mass grave or else their bodies were allowed to rot or be consumed by predatory beasts. This too has an apologetic value to Christians trying to defend their faith as politically non-subversive in the empire, in Mark's time. (b) Pilate's consent shows clearly that he was satisfied as to Jesus' real death. The burial was tantamount to a death certificate. Therefore, if Jesus was known to be alive after Easter day, it must be by a resurrection, since it is clear that he was killed and buried in a grave. The insertion of the clause "he was buried" in the first Christian credo (1 Cor 15:4) and the later Apostles' Creed has a similar apologetic thrust. The earliest Christian "heresy" was docetism, a denial of a real death of Jesus as well as his true incarnation as man.

These are the two elements of theological weight in Joseph's action, and can be joined in any sermon on what he did. A third "point" can be the man's courageous stand, after earlier records of his vacillation and secret discipleship. Joseph's character may be presented in the following ways: (1) a good man made better; (2) a wealthy man made richer; (3) a secret disciple made bold.

Every Day is Easter
(Mark 16:1–8)

The women of the gospel story were last at the cross (15:40-47) and they were first at the tomb. It is striking that these three faithful women play such a prominent role in discovering and announcing the resurrection of Jesus. Today we accept it as natural that women should appear alongside men in the gospel story, especially in light of Paul's teaching in Gal 3:26-28. But for the Jews then who had such a low opinion of a woman's status, especially in religious matters, the role of the women should have seemed shocking, even scandalous. But it is part of the scandal of the gospel in the first century.

The Jews believed that no woman's testimony in a lawcourt could be trusted. In fact she was not eligible to give evidence. Yet we find the consistent picture of women who in early Christianity gave the first news that Jesus was risen. There must have been a reason for this embarrassing datum in the gospel tradition; and it seems to be that from the beginning Christians have known of the women's testimony. There is the "ring of truth" about their amazed reports.

The content of what they reported and what was later verified was "Jesus is alive." Our gospel which breaks off suddenly at 16:8a offers us three grounds on which this claim rests. The preaching of the living Lord from Mark can use these three statements.

The Empty Tomb

When the women decided to come back at the close of the sabbath to anoint his body, they were in for a shock. The grave was open and the body of Jesus gone, with the rock at the mouth of the cave pushed over. The circular stone, used to seal the grave, had been rolled over, as visitors to Jerusalem today can see in a Herodian grave-site, near the King David Hotel, which has a "rolling stone" entrance. Jesus' grave was open—but not exactly empty. Jesus was not there, but there was a "young man, dressed in white, seated at the right side" (v. 5). Who he was is anybody's guess, and there have been several conjectures, including Theodor Zahn's notion that it was John Mark himself. Probably we are intended to recognize an angel (as in Acts 1:10). What is more important is what he said: "He is risen. He is not here: see the place where they laid him."

There is also a mild reproof in his words. "You are *seeking* Jesus of Nazareth." We recall that this verb is always used in Mark in a pejorative sense. So the angel is accusing the women of failing to believe Jesus' promise that he would be raised. They have come to the wrong place to find only a dead Jesus. He is not in the grave but on the road of life, and specifically he is in Galilee where his activity began and where it will be continued (14:28). Here is a starter for a sermon on "Seeking Christ in the Wrong Place" whether in a tomb or in our past experience or simply confined to "holy places." He always goes on ahead of us in the business of daily living.

The Appearances

William Barclay *(Crucified and Crowned* [London: SCM Press, 1961] pp. 165–70) has demonstrated how wide-ranging and varied are the resurrection appearances, with each appearance having a special purpose. Yet the single feature that runs through each narrative in the four gospels is the reality of Jesus' living presence that inspired devotion, trust and obedience. However we may want to "explain" the appearances and try to find a basis for what the disciples saw in terms of controlled visions and auditions, natural phenomena used by God, or even ESP, the most important element in the stories is the objectivity of the appearances—there was something there, or better, someone there, for them to see and touch and listen to, as Luke 24:39 says.

But Mark records no direct appearance. All the young man offers is the promise, "He is going before you into Galilee; there you will see him." We notice a characteristic Markan theme: Jesus is known in service as he resumes his former activity but now in the work and witness of his people. This is Mark's "proof" of the resurrection. Christ is still at work in Galilee where he began (1:14, 28), where he sent out the Twelve (3:14–15), and where he is still active.

The Promises

"As he told you" makes good the promise of Jesus in 14:28; the phrase clamps together the Jesus of the Passion and the risen Lord of glory. At his death, it was like a shepherd being killed and his flock dispersed. Now the shepherd comes back to seek and lead out his sheep. "He is going before you" recalls the scene of John 10:4.

So the promise of a reunion is renewed in Galilee. What Jesus continues to do—with his truth "let loose in all the world," as John Masefield's play dramatizes—has never been better described than in 16:20: "They went forth and preached everywhere, *the Lord working with them.*" Mark's story is the gospel of action, then and now.

Afterword

At the conclusion of our study of Mark's Gospel it may be repeated that this account of Jesus' earthly life and ministry holds a distinctive place in the NT library. In this the first of the gospels to be written, according to the traditional way of relating the four gospels, the accent falls again and again on Jesus as both divine son and human figure. The reason for this strange paradox has been explained in different ways. But what seems clear is the evangelist's intention to answer some false emphases in the early church which denied Jesus' true humanity and cast doubt on his sonship as involving a commitment to suffer and die. Above all, Jesus is pictured as a man of action, eagerly embracing his chosen destiny as God's agent to bring in his kingdom and to call his followers to engage with him in a mission to promote that rule of God in the world.

So this "Gospel" is eminently practical, and (true to its name, given in 1:1 and elsewhere, e.g., 1:14, 15; 8:35; 10:29; 13:10; 14:9) is intended to awaken faith and confirm wavering believers in their trust centered in the son of God.

Two illustrations, drawn from our lifetime, focus on the way Mark's Gospel has proven itself a turning-point in the encounter between God and the seeker after truth.

One such person was Anthony Bloom, archbishop of the Russian Orthodox Church. As a student in Paris he had lost his faith. He was persuaded, however, to hear a lecture on Christ and Christianity. He tells the result:

> I hurried home in order to check the truth of what the lecturer had been saying. I asked my mother whether she had a book of the gospels because I wanted to know whether the gospel would support the monstrous impression I had derived from this talk. I expected nothing good from my reading, so I counted the chapters of the four gospels to be sure that I read the shortest, not to waste time unnecessarily. And

thus it was the gospel according to St Mark which I
began to read. I do not know how to tell you what happened. I will put it quite simply and those of you who
have gone through a similar experience will know
what came to pass. While I was reading the beginning
of St Mark's gospel, before I reached the third chapter,
I was aware of a presence. I saw nothing. I heard nothing. It was no hallucination. It was a simple certainty
that the Lord was standing there and that I was in the
presence of him whose life I had begun to read with
such revulsion and such ill-will.

The second person is of another background and outlook.
The layperson John Lawrence had been brought up in a liberal Christian Family and in the Episcopal Church. Then came a
new chapter in his life:

When the last glow (of faith) had faded from the hori-
zon, the world seemed by contrast inexpressibly cold
and dreary. I was actually unhappy for a short time.
Then I considered the fact that if nothing was proved,
equally nothing was disproved. Ought I not to look
again at Christian belief? So I got out my Greek Testament and began to read St Mark's gospel, a few verses a
day. When I was about half way through I began to ask
myself, 'Who then was Jesus?' Was he more than a
man? After that I was over the top of the hill.

These two examples (taken from the story of their pil-
grimage in R. E. Davies [ed.], *We Believe In God* [London:
Allen and Unwin] pp. 26, 115; I owe this reference to Fr. Mark
Gibbard) are typical and could be added to. They serve to
show at least one thing: Mark's Gospel—and the Jesus it so
powerfully proclaims and portrays—has potential in our day
to appeal to and change human lives. Not surprisingly it has
been called "the life which was the Life of men" and women
(Laurence Housman).

Bibliography

Below are some of the current titles on the Gospel of Mark that are likely to be of most help to the preacher.

Commentaries

Anderson, Hugh, *The Gospel of Mark* (New Century Bible; Grand Rapids: Wm. B. Eerdmans, 1976).

Barclay, William, *The Gospel of Mark* (Daily Study Bible; Philadelphia: The Westminster Press, 1975).

Cranfield, C. E. B., *The Gospel According to St. Mark* (Cambridge Greek Testament Commentary; Cambridge: University Press, 1959).

Johnson, Sherman E., *Commentary on the Gospel of St. Mark* (Harper's NT Commentaries; New York: Harper and Row, 1972).

Lane, William L., *Commentary on the Gospel of Mark* (New International Commentary; Grand Rapids: Wm. B. Eerdmans, 1974).

Nineham, D. E., *Saint Mark* (Westminster Pelican Commentaries; Philadelphia: The Westminster Press, 1963).

Schmid, J., *Mark* (Regensburg NT; Cork: Mercier Press, 1968).

Schweizer, E., *Good News According to Mark* (Atlanta: John Knox, 1970).

Taylor, Vincent, *The Gospel According to St. Mark* (London: Macmillan, 1952).

Other Studies

Achtemeier, Paul J., *Mark* (Proclamation Commentaries; Philadelphia: Fortress Press, 1975).

Hultgren, Arland J., *Jesus and His Adversaries* (Minneapolis: Augsburg Publishing House, 1979).

Kee, Howard C., *Community of the New Age* (Philadephia: The Westminster Press, 1977).

Martin, Ralph P., *Mark: Evangelist and Theologian* (Grand Rapids: Zondervan, 1972).

Marxsen, Willi, *Mark the Evangelist* (Nashville: Abingdon Press, 1969).

Trocmé, Etienne, *The Formation of the Gospel According to Mark* (Philadelphia: The Westminster Press, 1975).